1,000,000 Books
are available to read at

www.ForgottenBooks.com

Read online
Download PDF
Purchase in print

ISBN 978-1-330-79591-0
PIBN 10106505

This book is a reproduction of an important historical work. Forgotten Books uses state-of-the-art technology to digitally reconstruct the work, preserving the original format whilst repairing imperfections present in the aged copy. In rare cases, an imperfection in the original, such as a blemish or missing page, may be replicated in our edition. We do, however, repair the vast majority of imperfections successfully; any imperfections that remain are intentionally left to preserve the state of such historical works.

Forgotten Books is a registered trademark of FB &c Ltd.
Copyright © 2018 FB &c Ltd.
FB &c Ltd, Dalton House, 60 Windsor Avenue, London, SW19 2RR.
Company number 08720141. Registered in England and Wales.

For support please visit www.forgottenbooks.com

1 MONTH OF FREE READING

at

www.ForgottenBooks.com

By purchasing this book you are eligible for one month membership to ForgottenBooks.com, giving you unlimited access to our entire collection of over 1,000,000 titles via our web site and mobile apps.

To claim your free month visit: www.forgottenbooks.com/free106505

* Offer is valid for 45 days from date of purchase. Terms and conditions apply.

English
Français
Deutsche
Italiano
Español
Português

www.forgottenbooks.com

Mythology Photography **Fiction** Fishing Christianity **Art** Cooking Essays Buddhism Freemasonry Medicine **Biology** Music **Ancient Egypt** Evolution Carpentry Physics Dance Geology **Mathematics** Fitness Shakespeare **Folklore** Yoga Marketing **Confidence** Immortality Biographies Poetry **Psychology** Witchcraft Electronics Chemistry History **Law** Accounting **Philosophy** Anthropology Alchemy Drama Quantum Mechanics Atheism Sexual Health **Ancient History** **Entrepreneurship** Languages Sport Paleontology Needlework Islam **Metaphysics** Investment Archaeology Parenting Statistics Criminology **Motivational**

THE LIFE AND TEACHING

OF

LEO TOLSTOY

THE WORKS OF LEO TOLSTOY.
Translated by Mr. and Mrs. AYLMER MAUDE.

THE REVISED EDITION OF THE WORKS OF LEO TOLSTOY.

EDITED BY AYLMER MAUDE.

Large crown 8vo, cloth gilt, 6s. each.

I.

Sevastopol, and other Military Tales. With Portrait, Map, Preface, and Transliteration Scheme.

XX.

Plays. With Illustrations, Preface, and List of Tolstoy's Works.

XXIV.

Resurrection. With Preface, Appendix, and 33 Illustrations by PASTERNÁK.

Resurrection. Cheaper Editions. Small crown 8vo, cloth, 2s. 6d. With PASTERNÁK's Illustrations; or without illustrations, 2s.

Essays and Letters (World's Classics, No. 46). Pott. 8vo, cloth gilt, 1s. net; buckram gilt, paper label, 1s. 6d. net. Leather, gilt top, side, and silk marker, 2s. net; parchment, gilt top and side, with silk marker, in case, 2s. 6d. net.

Esarhaddon, and other Tales. With an Introduction containing Letters by TOLSTOY, and a New Portrait. Fcap. 8vo, sewed, 6d.

POPULAR EDITIONS.

Demy 8vo, sewed, 6d. each.

Resurrection. Fifth Impression, completing 250,000 copies.

Sevastopol, and other Military Tales.

Tolstoy and his Problems. Essays by AYLMER MAUDE. Second Edition. Crown 8vo, cloth, 2s.; paper, 1s.

What is Art? By LEO TOLSTOY. Translated from the Original MS. With an Introduction by AYLMER MAUDE. Fcap. 8vo, paper covers, designed, 1s. net.

THE LIFE AND TEACHING

OF

LEO TOLSTOY

A BOOK OF EXTRACTS

With an Introduction

BY

G. H. PERRIS

CHEAP EDITION

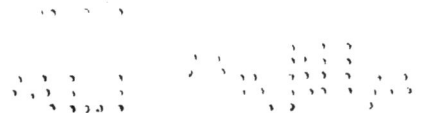

London

GRANT RICHARDS

48 LEICESTER SQUARE, W.C.

FIRST EDITION, *November*, 1901.
SECOND EDITION, *June*, 1904.

IN MEMORIAM

CONTENTS

CHAP.		PAGE
	INTRODUCTION	1
	ACKNOWLEDGMENT	47
I.	AUTOBIOGRAPHICAL AND DESCRIPTIVE	49

i. Youth—ii. Soldier, Landlord, Artist—iii. Conversion—iv. *Contra Mundum*.

II.	SOCIETY	96

i. The State in an Age of Violence—ii. Property, Luxury, and the Exploitation of Labour—iii. Some Proposed Remedies.

III.	THE GREAT COMMANDMENTS	139

i. The Law of Reason—ii. The Law of Peace, or Non-Resistance by Force—iii. The Law of Labour—iv. The Law of Purity—v. The Law of Sacrifice.

IV.	SCIENCE, FALSE AND TRUE	182
V.	ART, FALSE AND TRUE	196
VI.	EDUCATION	226
VII.	RELIGION	239

i. The New Life-Conception—ii. The Place of Ethics—iii. God—iv. Sins and Snares—v. Scripture, The Church, Prayer—vi. The Meaning of Life—vii. Hereafter.

The Life and Teaching of Leo Tolstoy

INTRODUCTION

THE genius of Leo Tolstoy speaks for itself. What I wish rather to emphasise in these introductory pages is the actuality and inevitability of the man and his gospel. Academic foot-rules are useless here; it is no armchair philosopher, *bombinans in vacuo,* no mere preacher of a school of doctrine, that we have before us. Tolstoy arises in a time of need out of the hard facts of life, as all the great prophets have done—as Moses, Jesus, Sakya Muni did in the ancient world. With ear close to earth and the popular heart, as the unwritten age-old songs of the peasantry are caught by the traveller, was this gospel of real life set down. Under the hand of the grand artist it takes form. As we consider it more, it seems like a pure diamond flashing forth the light of heaven in a single piercing beam or a prism of many colours. In essentials as old as the human conscience, it is yet the last lesson of human experience; in the courts of the Babylonian kings, the Pharaohs, the despots of the hoary East, in Pilate's hall, in the arena at Rome, in the dungeons of the Inquisition, the Star Chamber, the Bastile, the fortress of SS. Peter and Paul, in the sweating dens of London and New York, it has 'made its proofs' and given its testimony to the indestructibility of the soul. Only the new applications seem strange amid the artificialities, the more refined cruelties and sins, of our modern western life. Then appears the prophet, mediator between what is and what may be, demonstrator of the ideal as the practical, the real, the inevitable; and suddenly we recognise that our present state can no more be final than was that of the Church before Luther or French society under the later Bourbons. Here stands Leo Tolstoy, then, the Luther and the Rousseau of our day, heralding a new reformation in religion, a new revolution in politics and social relations. We have the privilege, but also the disadvantage, of watching him at comparatively close quarters as contemporaries. Let us anticipate the hardest scientific tests, and consider him in relation to his environment: the wonder of what he has already effected will be the greater. We see him, with feet always firmly planted on the Russian earth, towering up into a rare cosmopolitan ether. The western Philistine shouts that he is one of those mad Russians, and supposes the matter settled. Thus his ancestors may have dismissed St. Francis as one of those mad Italians, Luther as one of those mad Germans, Rousseau as one of those mad (and immoral) Frenchmen. In the qualities and circumstances that make him an incarnation of what is best in Russia, the point of incandescence of the Russian genius, I see, on the contrary, a guarantee of reality and permanence. And inasmuch as this 'New Testament country' may be said to be situate between east and west, between an old and a new social order, we have a conjunction of still larger, if hardly calculable, significance.

Count Lyoff Nicholaievitch Tolstoy was born very near the geographic centre of European Russia, in the region where the gloomy forests begin to merge into the rich wheat-lands of the south, in the year 1828—that is to say, seven years after the death of Napoleon, three years after the suppression of the ill-starred 'Decembrist' revolt in St. Petersburg and the accession of Nicholas I., two years before Comte's *Philosophie Positive* and the opening of the Liverpool-Manchester railway, and four years before the first English Reform Act and the deaths of Bentham and Goethe—a long period indeed in the west, but one that has seen fewer changes in Russia, where factory-industry and the new finance are only now beginning to make serious inroads upon the old rural life. Having lost his father, a military man, and his mother, a sweet being of whom we catch glimpses in his early writings, before he was well out of the nursery, his precocious and morbid mind was from the first burdened with the inheritance of a decrepit aristocracy. Compare the environment of his childhood with that of the southern states of America about the same time, and you realise how badly Russia has been injured by the success of the Tsars in repressing all independence and originality in the small noble class. Tolstoy is one of many 'repentant noblemen' in Russia—a singular phenomenon, due not simply to the strong strain of spirituality in the Slavic character, but also to the fact that under the autocratic régime aristocracy has had no genuine *raison d'être* whatever. Under the military · despotism of Nicholas I. public life offered no opportunity for an honest man. Criticism of the Government was crushed out unmercifully, and every sign of free intelligence brought down the heavy heel of the administration. After the many failures of '48 there was despair throughout Europe, but it was deepest of all in Russia. There have been many men of genius in the Empire during the second half of the century — great poets, novelists, critics, musicians, painters, economists, scientists—and few of them have escaped martyrdom. During all this time the sort of social and political activity which is the reasonable ambition of intelligent youth in the west has been absolutely impossible. Hence, Russia is the only European State in which an avowedly revolutionary movement is maintained, and in which anarchism is a widespread school of thought. Whatever we may think of the unlettered peasants, there is not, and never has been, any question about the capacity of the Russians of the educated class; yet they are almost as impotent in politics as the Ottoman Turk or the Asiatic native, and in the whole field of social endeavour and enterprise they are subject to the most brutal and stupid restrictions and penalties. It is impossible thus to cripple a great community without producing, even in the minds of its most capable members, all sorts of morbid developments.

Tolstoy was by birth over-sensitive and introspective; and all the circumstances of his youth —the hollow conditions of the society in which his guardians lived, and its helplessness under the autocratic reaction that led straight to the disasters of the Crimean War—helped to deepen these traits. Precocious, keenly observant, impatient of discipline and formal learning, awkward and bashful, always brooding, he was a sceptic at fifteen, and left the University of Kazan, in disgust at the stupid conventions of the time and place, without taking his degree. *Childhood, Boyhood, and Youth*—which appeared in three sections between 1852 and 1857—tells the story of this period, though the figure of Irtenieff is probably a projection rather than a portrait of himself, to whom he is always less fair, not to say merciful, than to others. This book is a most uncompromising exercise in self-analysis. It is of great length, there is no plot, and few outer events are recorded. The realism is often morbid, but is varied by some passages of great descriptive power, such as the account of the storm, and occasionally by tender pathos, as in the story of the soldier's death, as well as by grimly vivid pages, such as the narrative of the mother's death. In this earliest work will be found the seeds both of Tolstoy's artistic genius and of his ethical gospel.

After five years of mildly benevolent efforts among his serfs at Yasnaya Polyana (the disappointments of which he related a few years later in *A Landlord's Morning*, intended to have been part of a full novel to be called *A Russian Proprietor*), his elder brother Nicholas persuaded him to join the army, and in 1851 he was drafted to the Caucasus as an artillery officer. On this favourite stage of classic Russian romance, where for the first time he saw the towering mountains and the tropical sun, and met the rugged, adventurous highlanders, Tolstoy felt his imagination stirred as Byron did among the isles of Greece, and his early revulsion against city life confirmed as Wordsworth did amid the lakes, and Thoreau at Walden, by a direct call from Nature to his own heart. The largest result of this experience was *The Cossacks* (1852). Turgenieff described this fine prose epic of the contact of civilised and savage man as 'the best novel written in our language.' *The Raid* (or *The Invaders*, as Mr. Dóle's translation is entitled), dating from the same year, *The Woodcutting Expedition* (1855), *Meeting an Old Acquaintance* (1856), and *A Prisoner in the Caucasus* (1862), are also drawn from recollections of this sojourn, and show the same descriptive and romantic power. Upon the outbreak of the Crimean War he was called to Sebastopol, where he had command of a battery and took part in the defence of the citadel. The immediate product of these dark months of bloodshed was the thrilling series of impressions reprinted from one of the leading Russian reviews as *Sebastopol Sketches* (1856). From that day onward Tolstoy knew and told the hateful truth about war and the thoughtless pseudo-patriotism which hurries nations into fratricidal slaughter. From that day there was expunged from his mind all the cheap romanticism which depends upon a glorification of the savage side of human nature. These wonderful pictures of the routine of the battlefield established his position in Russia as a writer, and later on created in western countries an impression like that made by the canvases of Verestchagin.

For a brief time Tolstoy became a figure in the old and new capitals of Russia by right of talent as well as birth. His chequered friendship with Turgenieff, one of the oddest chapters in literary history, can only be mentioned here. In 1857 he travelled in Germany, France, and Italy. It was of these years that he declared in *My Confession* that he could not think of them without horror, disgust, and pain of heart. The catalogue of crime which he charged against himself in his salvationist crisis of twenty years later must not be taken literally; but that there was some ground for it we may guess from the scenic and incidental realism of the *Recollections of a Billiard-marker* (1856), and of many a later page. Several other powerful short novels date from about this time, including *Albert* and *Lucerne*, both of which remind us of Tolstoy's susceptibility to music; *Polikushka*, a tale of peasant life; and *Family Happiness*, the story of a marriage that failed, a most clear, consistent, forceful, and in parts beautiful piece of work, anticipating in essentials *The Kreutzer Sonata*, that was to scandalise the world thirty years later.

After all, it was family happiness that saved Leo Tolstoy. For the third time the hand of death had snatched away one of the nearest to him—his brother Nicholas. Two years later, in 1862, he married Miss Behrs, daughter of an army surgeon in Tula—the most fortunate external event in his whole life, I should think. Family responsibilities, those novel and daring experiments in peasant education which are recorded

INTRODUCTION 9

in several volumes of the highest interest, the supervision of the estate, magisterial work, and last, but not least, the prolonged labours upon *War and Peace* and *Anna Karènina*, fill up the next fifteen years. *War and Peace* (1864–69) is a huge panorama of the Napoleonic campaign of 1812, with preceding and succeeding episodes in Russian society. These four volumes display in their superlative degree Tolstoy's indifference to plot and his absorption in individual character; they are rather a series of scenes, threaded upon the fortunes of several families, than a set novel, but they contain passages of penetrating psychology and vivid description, as well as some suggestions toward an anarchist philosophy of history. Of this work, which carried its author's fame into the west, Flaubert (how the name carries us backward!) wrote, 'It is of the first order. What a painter, and what a psychologist! The two first volumes are sublime, but the third drags frightfully. There are some quite Shakespearean things in it.' The artist's hand was now strengthening for his highest attainment. In 1876 appeared *Anna Karènina*, his greatest and, as he intended at the time (but Art is not so easily jilted), his last novel. The fine qualities of this book, which, though long, is dramatically unified and vitally coherent, have been so fully recognised that I need not attempt to describe them. Mr. George Meredith has described Anna as 'the most perfectly depicted female character in all fiction,' which, from the author of *Diana*, is praise indeed. Parallel with the main subject of the illicit love of Anna and Vronsky there is a minor subject in the fortunes of Levine and Kitty, wherein the reader will discover many of Tolstoy's own experiences. Matthew Arnold complained that the book contained too many characters and a burdensome multiplicity of actions, but praised its author's extraordinarily fine perception and no less extraordinary truthfulness, and frankly revelled in Anna's 'large, fresh, rich, generous, delightful nature.'

Settled for good on the paternal estate, among the *mujiks* whom he had always loved, the deeper questions of life were stilled, but not extinguished, by the pressure and the comfort of immediate duties. His mind reflected the unsettlement of a time when religion as by law and power established was everywhere shaking under the blows of physical science, a time of especial unsettlement in Russian life. In speaking of these days Tolstoy always pictures himself as wandering in the arid desert of materialistic scepticism; but to us the ethical bias of his mind is apparent throughout his work. A diet of physics and philanthropy could not for ever satisfy a soul so strenuous. In *Anna Karènina* Levine says, 'I am going to enrich medicine with a new term—the labour cure. It is a sovereign specific against nervous troubles.' In over-laborious England the idea had been familiarised twenty years before by

Carlyle; but I have no reason to suppose that Tolstoy was influenced by the stern sage of Craigenputtock and Chelsea. Indeed, the historical anarchism which he worked out at such portentous length in *War and Peace* is the exact antithesis of the philosophy of *Heroes and Hero-Worship.* Tolstoy's 'labour cure' sprang from the exigencies of his situation—the needs of a growing family, and of that larger peasant family which required sympathetic and skilled leadership more than ever after the Emancipation. It was, and is, directed rather to the idle rich than to the ignorant poor; and if 'labour' has with Tolstoy nearly always and exclusively meant useful agricultural labour—'bread-work,' as he called it later on—he has distinctly warned his readers against 'the idolatry of labour,' and a fine balance of mental and manual activity has been presumed in his preaching as clearly as it has been shown in his life for the last forty years. The period of his 'discovery of the "labour cure,"' which for him meant actually sharing the toil of his field-hands, was the period wherein he accomplished his largest and his finest imaginative productions. It was the time also when he carried out his quaint essays in anarchist schooling. He admitted their failure afterwards; the educational world has yet to learn their full value. For a short time, too, he was occupied as a district magistrate; he made studies in scientific agriculture; he was a model father and husband, and an enthusiastic sportsman. *Anna Karènina*, which was completely published in 1876, won him not only the highest place among Russian literary artists, but a seat among the world's immortals.

Then came the shock of his 'conversion.' The artist, so far from respecting his laurels, had chosen the moment of supreme honour as the occasion of most utter self-abasement. There were to be no more novels, no more plays; the master-artist had 'got religion.' Henceforth there would be nothing for him but the gospel. It is difficult for us to realise the effect of *My Confession* on the educated class in Russia, whose praise was thus scorned and turned to naught, because it is difficult for us to realise a condition of society in which, for that class, religion has been so far starved and persecuted out of existence by the allied powers of State and Church. In the early eighties the new non-conformist sects in Russia, like the Stundists and Dukhobortsi, had scarcely begun to take the dimensions they have since reached. No one thought of the possibility of an effective religious revolt against the autocracy. Tolstoy himself never put such an idea into words. Yet he was very much in earnest. 'When I had ended my work *Anna Karènina*,' he said in *My Confession* (1879-82), 'my despair reached such a height that I could do nothing but think of the horrible condition in which I found myself. . . . I saw only one thing—death. Everything else was a lie.' The critics everywhere took him at his word, and managed to get the episode quite out of focus with the facts of the man's history and environment. So you would gather to this day from a certain type of writer that there are really two Tolstoys—the artist whose work was closed in 1876, and the preacher who has since bored the world with dubious theology and an impossible moral code. If he had ceased his activities, say, in 1884—by which time his criticism of Greek Orthodox theology, his reconstruction of the Gospels, and *My Religion* had been produced—it is to be feared that this false idea would have gone down into history. It is easy to get a truer view to-day. *The Death of Ivan Ilyitch* (1884), *The Kreutzer Sonata* (1889), *Master and Man* (1895), and the extraordinarily powerful story *Resurrection* (1900)—to name only a few of the works that have flowed from his fertile pen in the meantime—effectually disposed of the notion that art and religion are mutually incompatible factors in the activity of genius. This, of course, does not mean that the 'conversion' is a negligible quantity in Tolstoy's history. On the contrary, it is highly significant and characteristic. But it was not quite the 'new fact' which his protestations would suggest to the superficial reader. It was new only in degree. The meeting with the peasant preacher Sutayeff, in 1879, was just the spark which fired his old faith in the *mujik* and in pure ethical motive-forces to the burning point. That faith was latent in his earliest writings; it sustained him in the disappointments of his country life; it broke forth in the person of Levine in his great novel. Now, at the meridian of fifty years, and in a fresh crisis in his country's development, a hunger fell upon him which neither art nor science nor the ordinary round of bodily toil could satisfy.

The life of a Tolstoy is not to be flattened out into the semblance of a map in which the course of every road and stream and coast-line is visible. But the coincidence of the acute period of his 'conversion' with the acute period of the revolutionary movement commonly but stupidly named 'Nihilism' is too suggestive to be overlooked. The large towns of Russia were in a state of civil war. Official terrorism had provoked the most desperate campaign of vengeance that any country had witnessed during the latter part of the nineteenth century. The prisons were full of political suspects and offenders; the salons echoed with stories of these horrible dens of filth, disease, and cruelty. The famous 'Executive Committee' loomed large in the popular imagination. Though the peasantry made but little response, it was no mere vendetta of a few malcontents. A very large part of the educated class was in revolt. Thousands of men and women, many of whom would have been honoured leaders of thought and social activity in any free country, were swept away to Siberia, to die a dog's death in the mines or among the half-savage natives of the sub-arctic zone. The very roots of moral order and progress were torn up; not a ray of hope illumined the future. Perturbation ruled to the point of nightmare in the minds of intelligent observers, and most of all, perhaps, in the minds of those few elect who, like Tolstoy, while honestly unable to side with either party in this violent struggle, yet vainly groped about for a third line of action. There is to be found at least one impulse towards the new departure marked by *My Confession.*

His subsequent ethical and religious development may be traced in a long series of books and pamphlets, of which the most important are— *The Gospels Translated, Compared, and Harmonised* (1880-2), *What I Believe* (*My Religion*), produced abroad in 1884, *What is to be Done?* (1884-5), *Life* (1887), *The First Step* (1892), *The Kingdom of God is within You* (1893), *Patriotism and Christianity* (1896), *The Christian Teaching* (1898), *What is Art?* (1898), *The Slavery of Our Times* (1900), *The Meaning of Life* (1901). In addition to these there are many smaller letters and articles on the successive famines and the religious persecutions in Russia, on social evils and remedies, and passages from private diaries on aspects of the personal religious life, most of which are available in the excellent cheap editions of the Free Age Press. From this friendly and authoritative source there has been poured of late a succession of booklets, pamphlets, and leaflets in which the great writer reaffirms, illustrates, amplifies the thoughts that have pretty consistently possessed him for the last fifty years. In all the vast flood of polemical literature and of pulpit eloquence there is nothing like these simple, direct, strenuous appeals to the thinking mind to direct itself to the realities of life. No doubt it is the spirit of the man, not any literal interpretation, that we need. But such is his pre-eminence, not only of aim but of power and interest, that there is nothing he has written that will not help the careful reader.

All the time, in this volcanic and fecund if fundamentally simple personality, the artist has dogged the steps of the evangelist. *Master and Man* (1895) is one of the most exquisite short stories ever written. *The Death of Ivan Ilyitch* (1884) is a powerful portrayal of the end of a Philistine. The much-condemned drama of peasant life, *The Dominion of Darkness* (1886), and *The Kreutzer Sonata* (1889), will be more fairly judged when the average Englishman has learned the merit of simple truthfulness in art. One stands aghast at the insolence with which the average professional critic treats a work like *Resurrection*. To submit such a book to the summary treatment which the ordinary novel receives and merits is absurd. Tolstoy is a man apart, standing head and shoulders above any living teacher and every living literary artist with one or two possible exceptions. Rarely in human

INTRODUCTION 17

history has there been an influence comparable with his. Yet this influence is only in the springtime of its increase. A century hence Tolstoy will be known as Milton and Bunyan and Dickens, perhaps even as Isaiah and Paul, Augustine and Shakespeare, are known. The column of newspaper twaddle in such a case is unusually futile. An English publisher, in a jocular mood one supposes, affixed to *Resurrection* a couple of pages of 'press notices.' They show that Mr. So-and-So, an intelligent reader, regards this as Tolstoy's 'greatest work.' Perhaps so; it is not so easy to judge between *War and Peace*, *The Cossacks*, *Family Happiness*, *Anna Karènina*, and *Resurrection*. In these altitudes the normal standards fail; and such comparisons seem to me to be peculiarly worthless in Tolstoy's case, because the same great qualities run through all his works from first to last. From *Childhood and Youth*, produced fifty years ago, downwards through the long catalogue, the same uncompromising veracity, the same extraordinary insight into the recesses of character, the same passionate yet tender humanism, the same dramatic skill conditioned by the same thirst after righteousness, are to be found. He is the same Tolstoy all the time, before and after the salvationist episodes of twenty years ago. The last lines of this novel are highly characteristic. Nekhlùdoff, the idle aristocrat, has realised his sin and tried to atone for it; he has brought unhappiness to many of the friends whom he leaves behind in the heartless and brainless society of his youth, some gleams of light into the lives of those whom he accompanies into prison and exile. The last romantic idea of his philanthropic period is broken when the peasant girl whom he has ruined and would help bravely refuses his sacrifice, and goes out to seek her own salvation. '" Scarcely have I finished one life," says Nekhlùdoff, " and another has commenced." And a perfectly new life dawned that night for Nekhlùdoff, not because he had entered into new conditions of life, but because everything he did after that night had a new and quite different significance. How this new period of his life will end, time alone will prove.' That is Tolstoy all over. All his great works have ended with a similar prospective note, and one has always a sense that the writer is looking forward to a yet further statement of the old radical problems, a new staging of the old drama, before the task is finished. With restless hand and an eye that sees externals and essentials with like accuracy and rapidity, the master paints his panorama of the fall and recovery of man. Because the dramatic quality of these pictures lies, not in their organisation in a conventionally limited plot, but, first, in the great moral idea upon which they are threaded, then in the life-likeness of individual characters, and ever and anon in the grip of particular episodes, the little critics scoff. The idea, the characters, the episodes, all shock their precious British self-complacency. One of them observes that

INTRODUCTION 19

'*Resurrection* is thoroughly bad art,' and then somewhat overshoots his mark by adding that 'it is as if written by Zola in collaboration with the Prophet Isaiah,' a collaboration for which, I imagine, the world would gladly sacrifice much of what passes for art in our decrepit societies. 'Benumbing influence of over-development of the ethical theory is remarkably conspicuous,' according to a leading literary journal. Tolstoy, it appears, is 'a precious vase which has been broken'; all we can do now with him is to glue the pieces together, and make him 'the ornament of a museum.' The *Oxford Review* bemoans 'the absence of clever dialogue, the lack of rhetoric, and utter want of softening touches.' If the supreme work of a Tolstoy—whose genius, now strengthened and refined by seventy years of strenuous life, is unquestionable—is to be smothered in this sort of rubbish, we may guess how little chance any younger or less robust talent has at the hands of our erstwhile 'fourth estate.'

The fact we have to recognise amid our diseased civilisation, as Tolstoy himself has had to do with his beloved peasants, is that there are thousands of 'good-natured' and 'intelligent' people who do not want to be good, to love their neighbour, to maintain themselves honestly; who do not want peace, do not want truth. Yes, above all, they do not want to know or speak the truth. So we find men who are in no way able to call his accuracy in question, and who do not dispute the sympathy and delicacy of his method, complaining that Tolstoy's subjects are repulsive and some of his scenes horrible. What they want in a novel is pleasure, and the moral evolution of a young *roué* and his victim, told as the archangel might tell it in the books of doom, is not pleasant. However innocent they may have thought themselves, there are too many old friends in this, at first sight, strange company of noblemen and officials, judges, advocates, and jurors, prostitutes and thieves, peasants, servants, revolutionists—too many people just like you and me—for their portrayal, just as they are, to give us the objective amusement we demand of Messrs. Mudie. Used to judging a book, we suddenly find a book judging us. With a very few microscopic exceptions, set there to remind us that our magician is but human after all, there is not a word of preaching from end to end; the Russians are men and brothers; the hero is neither a coxcomb nor a ranter; Maslova wins us in spite of her demoralisation. The morality is intrinsic; it is that, not of the pulpit, but of real life, a growth out of the coarse soil. The thing is told as it was. As we read, the eyes of a god seem to be upon us, pitilessly searching; the voice of a god with inexorable tenderness whispers, 'Thou art the man!' To awakened minds this is the most precious of gifts. For a septuagenarian, *Resurrection* is an almost unparalleled *tour de force;* we can hardly hope that it will be surpassed.

INTRODUCTION 21

It crowns an already immense achievement. Tolstoy is one, of the most prolific writers of a prolific century. He has written something like fifty full books, and innumerable fragments. At first sight there is little variety of subject-matter or scenery. Yet, what compensation when we get below the surface, behind the scenery, to the play of character! what wonderful insight into the tragedy of the human soul! No other modern writer, Shakespeare himself only occasionally, gives one this sense of absolute knowledge of the secrets hidden away in the innermost chambers of the mind, and of absolute honesty in their exposure. This perennial interest in the depths of character and in the elemental and crucial questions of conduct, this extreme honesty of speech, seem to me to be the most precious qualities of modern Russian literature. In giving us the rarest presentation of them, Tolstoy reveals to us, so that he who runs may read, the genius of a people too long unknown or misrepresented—a people destined in the future to play a part in the world's history greater, perhaps, than the most ardent Panslavists have dreamed of. When Turgenieff, writing from his death-bed, begged his friend to 'return to literature,' he took, for once, a narrow view of character and destiny. Genius must work itself out on its own lines. Tolstoy remained a Russian from tip to toe—that is one of his supreme values for us. And he remained an indivisible personality. The artist and the moralist are inseparable in his works. 'We are not to take *Anna Karènina* as a work of art,' said Matthew Arnold; 'we are to take it as a piece of life.' The distinction is not very satisfactorily stated, but the meaning is clear. So, too, W. D. Howells, in his introduction to an American edition of the *Sebastopol Sketches*, 'I do not know how it is with others to whom these books of Tolstoy's have come, but for my part I cannot think of them as literature in the artistic sense at all. Some people complain to me, when I praise them, that they are too long, too diffuse, too confused, that the characters' names are hard to pronounce, and that the life they portray is very sad and not amusing. In the presence of these criticisms I can only say that I find them nothing of the kind, but that each history of Tolstoy's is as clear, as orderly, as brief as something I have lived through myself. . . . I cannot think of any service which imaginative literature has done the race so great as that which Tolstoy has done in his conception of Karènina at that crucial moment when the cruelly outraged man sees that he cannot be good with dignity. This leaves all tricks of fancy, all effects of art, immeasurably behind.'

His service to literature is, in fact, precisely the same as his service to morals. Like Bunyan and Burns, Dickens and Whitman, he throws down in a world of decadent conventions the gage of the democratic ideal. As he calls the politician and the social reformer back to the land and the common people, so he calls the artist back to the elemental forces ever at work beneath the surface-show of nature and humanity. To exceptional insight and sincerity he adds that absolute simplicity of manner which we generally associate with genius. He is a realist, not of the outer, but of the inner life. There is no staginess, no sentimentality, in his work. He has no heroes in our western sense—none, even, of those sensational types of personality which glorify the name of his northern contemporary Ibsen. His style is always natural, direct, irresistible as a physical process. He has rarely strayed beyond the channel of his own experience, and the reader who prefers breadth to depth of knowledge must seek elsewhere. He has little humour, but a grimly satiric note has sometimes crept into his writing, as Archdeacon Farrar will remember. Of artifice designed for vulgar entertainment he knows nothing; in the world of true art, which is the wine-press of the soul of man, he is a princely figure.

Such is the man whom I have ventured in another place to describe as 'The Grand Mujik,' because his qualities seemed to me to be the qualities of the best Russian peasant type carried up to the point of genius. It is, if I see it aright, an untutored, irregular, persistent, volcanic genius; hardly capable of finished, judicial self-expression; shrewd, naïve, impetuous, yet wonderfully consistent from first to last; immensely fertile and suggestive; incapable of trickery; always responsive, amid its ceaseless tides of emotion, to certain fundamental moral interests and principles; concentrated more and more as youth passes upon the two desperate problems, 'What is the meaning of life?' and 'What, then, is to be done?'

Tolstoyism, as it has been elaborated during these later years, is neither theology nor philosophy nor scholarship as we commonly understand those terms. It is rather a moral code, as exacting as can be formulated by a sane and eminently practical man, yet simple enough for all to understand, and as inspiring and bracing as it is simple. Reason and Love — these are its two eternal pillars. The essence of Tolstoy's religion is a complete faith in the efficiency of these two immeasurable forces; its most striking characteristic, as compared with the armchair philosophies of the day, is its insistent association of faith and works, precept and practice. It appeals not to controversial tests, not to any appearance of 'sweet reasonableness,' but to actual trial in the rough and tumble of daily life; and it will accept no other judgment. I have attempted to summarise its practical and critical side in a five-fold commandment—a warning against dogma, mysticism, ceremonial hypnotism, the binding of the mind and will by oaths, and other inventions of external authority in religion and politics, or the law of Reason; a warning against participation in violence, individual or social, and organisations dependent on violence, or the law of Peace; a warning against exploitation, luxury, and material property, or the law of Labour; a warning against self-degradation, or the law of Purity; and, finally, a warning against devotion to self, or the law of Sacrifice. It is impossible here fully to discuss even the more challenging of these articles of faith; but a few words must be said in regard to two of them—the principle of non-resistance, so-called, and the general political implications of Tolstoy's Christian anarchism; and the principle of bread-labour, as worked out into an indictment of our whole industrial system and the social relations based on it.

The word 'non-resistance' is unhappy. Tolstoy is very far from being a quietist. No prophet has told the truth in the very citadel of lies with more boldness or with more scathing analytic power. What Tolstoy recommends is not submission, but moral resistance. For the first time in the modern world, adequate expression has been given in his writings and in his life to the enormous possibilities of resisting tyranny and cruelty without blood-guiltiness. The spectacle of this single man defying the whole armed strength of the Tsardom, and speaking to the world from a little village in the heart of Russia, has a grandeur equalled by few things in human history. I said at the outset that the qualities in which he is essentially Russian, so far from providing an excuse for neglecting or minimising his teaching, give an additional reason for the gravest consideration, and this for two reasons. In the first place, his teaching is no invention of the study or school, no mere product of that unreal, irresponsible condition which we call genius and associate with insanity; it is the rare essence of popular wisdom, distilled during centuries of labour and suffering. And, secondly, at this moment it is standing the sternest practical tests. The struggle against despotism will appeal to the best instincts of mankind so long as despotism remains, and the Russian revolutionist has been a peculiarly heroic figure. But he must indeed be blind who, looking back over the history of the last century, fails to see that violent methods have rarely, if ever, done permanent service to the popular cause, that force is in the long-run always on the side, not of the big battalions of the people, but on that of the small battalions of the autocrats, plutocrats, and aristocrats. Tolstoy reminds us, in phrases which are a sort of moral dynamite, that there are modes of revolutionary activity which have yet to be fully tried, and which, when they are put to the test by a whole people, or even a large number of them, may yield some astonishing results. The Irish 'no-rent' campaign collapsed because the Irish people are comparatively deficient in that capacity for silent, dogged endurance which the *mujik* possesses in a very high degree. If for 'non-resistance' we read passive or moral resistance, possibilities arise, which, as between a hundred million peasants and a hundred thousand officials, give ground for hoping that the last word of popular right has not yet been said. The failure—if such it can be called—of the Dukhobortsi is no worse than the failure of the conspirators of twenty years ago; and history records as many victories for liberty won at the martyrs' stake as on the battlefield. This is not merely a Russian lesson. As Russia under the Tsars is a lurid illustration, of militarism, imperialism, and administrative authority in their *ultima ratio*, so Tolstoy has become the extreme embodiment of the reaction against diseased developments which are common, though in different degree, to the whole western world—the triumphs of money and machinery, and the justifying theories to which they have given birth. Tolstoy insists more than once upon the importance of taking social evils in the order of their real gravity; his part has been to show that, after a century's struggle against poverty on the part of humane people, not poverty but violence, not political and economic, but moral inequality, are the worst evils which block the way to a happier order. For the purpose of these few sentences I shall take it for granted that the reader agrees with me in regarding Tolstoy's indictment of society as it stands as being, in the main, accurate. As to his prescriptions, I will not here go farther than to insist that the only criticisms that have any moral value are those which rest upon a prior appreciation. No moral formula that man has ever devised is quite beyond question, but we have the right to demand that any critic of the great commandments shall have appreciated their strength before he expects us to listen to his statement of their weakness. If this procedure be applied to the principle of 'non-resistance' as it is re-stated by the great Russian teacher, we shall be on the way to the truth. Once get men to admit, on the one hand, the waste and cruelty of force, as we see it all around us, and, on the other hand, the enormous effectiveness of the moral influence which Tolstoy's life exemplifies as well as his works inculcate it, and criticisms will fall into their natural place. Take, for instance, the familiar argument that violence must be justifiable when used to restrain violence—the violence of the would-be murderer or adulterer is the stock example. What must strike the open-minded man, in the first place, is the unreality of the case in point; an exceedingly rare incident which appeals to generous emotion is being used to buttress the use of force in cases of daily occurrence which make no such appeal to the better instincts. We might as well quote the unhappy experience of a given man or woman against monogamy in general, or in favour of easy divorce. It will hardly be denied that a prejudice against the use of force is of the essence of civilisation. If, instead of darkening counsel with the discussion of ultimate questions, and raising logical stumbling-blocks in the way of the weaker brethren, we were taking care in the common junctures of our daily life that, so far as possible, our bias and influence should be on the side of love and peace, and against that of force and purely external authority, the whole social outlook would be lightened. At present the bias of the great majority of men on the great majority of occasions is on the side of force and authority; and the settlement of social life, the elaboration of the industrial system, and the daily wider ramification of governmental organisation tend more and more to attenuate the old faith in moral influence and voluntary co-operation. It used to be said, without risk of denial, that 'The blood of the martyrs is the seed of the Church.' Now, I find an honoured leader of the peace movement, a man whose life is one long testimony to the efficacy of moral influence, falling to the sceptical objection that 'If a righteous and useful man allow himself to be murdered by a scoundrel on the ground that one man's life is as sacred as that of another, the result would be the triumph of evil over good.' Logically pursued, this would mean that all good and heroic lives have been vain and mistaken, because they have been continually thwarted by scoundrels.

Tolstoy's position is that the 'ground' which necessitates a certain view of things—the condition of mind for which all lives seem equally sacred—is more important than the destiny of the bodily life itself; that if you believe the hypothetical scoundrel's life to be sacred—sacred because potentially good—no personal inconvenience and no appearance of a triumph of evil can justify your killing him; that you never can be sure even of an immediate and relative good coming of violence; that the only real triumph of evil is the good man's betrayal of his principles; that the greatest turning-points, the most influential events of history, are the martyrdoms of good men by scoundrels. And as to the extension of this plea into a fear of nations 'foremost in wisdom and in usefulness' being 'extinguished by savages and barbarians,' who can tell us which nation is wise and which savage? Does it not come to this, that no nation should kill any other nation, and no individual any other individual? If we are going to claim that there may be some exceptions to this rule, or at least some cases in which violence is comparatively excusable, it is still the rule, not the exception, we should emphasise. It is, I repeat, the emphasis that is all-important. By men who do not, and perhaps do not wish to, understand him, Tolstoy is generally condemned as a dreamer. In fact, he is intensely practical. The theoretical question whether violence is in any case morally justifiable may never be settled; at any rate, it is not settled in the mind of the present writer.

The practical, immediate, and momentous question whether the violence and the worship of external authority that fill our daily lives are good or bad, on the whole, may be settled at once and decisively by any man who can use his eyes, ears, and brain. And the fulfilment of the simple moral requirement will work a revolution, both in our individual and our social life, large enough to satisfy the most exalted ambition of the twentieth century.

So much said—the waste, injustice, and general ineffectiveness of force being supposed to be admitted—we may attempt to decide in which fields the application of this principle is more and in which it is less urgently required. Here history gives us plain guidance. Whereas the growth of a State means the modification of violence, the suppression of its crudest forms, within a certain area, States in their mutual relations lag far behind in this pacific development. This arrest, or even reversion to the savagery of ancient times, takes two special forms in our day, according as the countries in question are equal or unequal in power. As between fairly equal nations or groups of nations we have the evils of militarism, or what is called the armed peace, which is a sort of permanent civil war in the general comity. As between strong and weak peoples we have the evils of imperialism, which is now, as it has been throughout history, the exploitation of feebler races by a camarilla of capitalists, aristocrats, officials, and soldiers, that has first become dominant in a powerful State. It is remarkable that the three clearest indictments of militarism in recent years have come from three Russians—Count Tolstoy, the Tsar Nicholas II. in his rescript of invitation to the Hague Conference, and M. Jean de Bloch in his theory of the 'impossibility' of modern warfare. Of these, Tolstoy's work is infinitely the most far-reaching. He knows by experience what war means; he rightly holds that, at bottom, imperialism is the same thing whether it has a Slavic or a Saxon name; and he exhibits militarism as the schooling of whole nations to mutual hatred, their perversion from domestic industry and reform to be the fighting serfs of small ruling classes who play with them as with pawns on a chess-board. Against the double evil he offers a great principle—the principle of internationalism, which has found in him its most thorough-going modern advocate, and a practical plan of campaign, the strike against military service. Here, again, I ask the reader to consider the truth and the practical importance of his teaching before he considers the occasional and minor perversities which mark its statement. There is truth even in those perversities. Take his contemptuous references to the Peace Movement, and such a passage as this from 'Letters on War':—

'If people who think little or but superficially were able to comfort themselves with the idea

INTRODUCTION 33

that international courts of arbitration would supersede wars and ever-increasing armaments, the Hague Conference and the war that followed it demonstrated in the most obvious manner the impossibility of finding a solution of the difficulty in that way. After the Hague Conference it became obvious that, as long as governments with armies exist, the termination of armaments and of wars is impossible. That an agreement should become possible it is necessary that the parties to it should trust each other. And in order that the Powers should trust each other they must lay down their arms.'

No nation has ever acted on this last precept, and yet, as Tolstoy himself contends, the mind of the nations has been continually advancing in the direction of general peace. The analogy of internal peace shows that disarmament may proceed very slowly, *pari passu* with the growth of mutual trust and the perception of common interests; and this trust and perception of community are in nothing more clearly shown than in the multiplication of public conferences and the increasing vogue of arbitration. To doubt the value of these new developments is to doubt the power of reason in social relations. The custom of arbitration, which in the last few years has entered so largely into our daily commercial life, is, even from the point of view of the high Tolstoyan ideal, a great advance upon appeals to the law; international arbitration has settled many grave disputes, it is being every year more widely practised, and the institution at the Hague of a permanent tribunal in which twenty-six independent states are represented will give a great stimulus to this attempt to substitute equity for brute force. But, when all this is said—when we have discounted Tolstoy's vigorous preconceptions, his anti-scientific bias, his peremptory temper, those traces of mother earth which cling to the freest brain, the bias of Slavic anarchism in the mind of this citizen of the world—there still remains a measure of truth which is of special moment to us westerners, who have become so thoroughly inoculated with faith in legislation and representation that we can hardly realise any possibility of effective individual action. In the first place, the governments will not abolish militarism of their own accord—they will, on the contrary, resist its abolition by every means in their power. If they agree to the limitation of warfare, it is because warfare as between the great white peoples has ceased to serve the purposes of the ruling caste. In the second place, the sort of propaganda that has been conducted by the peace societies, with excellent spirit and not without success, in the past century is only too evidently unequal to the needs of the situation. Only when the pacific movement had a Gladstone or a Bright at its head did it attain really popular proportions; but we seem to have passed beyond this heroic period in our political history. The word of to-morrow is democracy. How, then, is the common man to secure peace? By union, we expect. It is here that Tolstoy comes in. 'You are threatened in England,' he might say, 'with conscription in some form. Not that the military system, as you have it, is morally much superior, since it depends upon the training of pauper boys under economic compulsion to the trade of human butchery. But let us admit that conscription would be a step backward. You propose to organise a national agitation through local organisations, mass meetings, and so on—an effort that will require great expenditure of labour and money, that will be misrepresented or boycotted by the press, and will provoke a counter-agitation which will have the support of the government, its political followers, and all the wealthy classes. How much more simply and effectively this evil could be dealt with! If the people do not object to military service they will not support your agitation; if they do, and if only a thousand young men are sufficiently in earnest to refuse either to be compelled or to be cajoled into barracks' slavery, and go to prison instead, there will soon be an end of the attempt to enforce military service, for a fire like this spreads quickly. A good many thousands of "ignorant" Russian peasants have set the example; if there are not even a thousand Englishmen earnest enough to follow it, what are we to think of your vaunted "freedom" and of the theory on which your political institutions are based?'

In some of the later pamphlets, the anarchist strain is pushed to a further extreme than is reached, except by implication, in Tolstoy's larger works. Hatred of all political organisation is, to say the least, more natural in a Russian than in an Englishman or Frenchman; and here we have not only the glorification of individual goodness and the indictment of society as it stands, with all its sins thick upon it, but some unsympathetic criticism of western humanitarian movements, and, finally, a radical objection to governments of every kind. 'Not only military governments but governments in general' are useless and harmful. The issue between voluntarism and the representative system opens long vistas of debate; and on many points the answer to Tolstoy is obvious. Governments could only be harmless, he says, 'if they consisted of immaculate, holy people.' But it is surely a legitimate retort that his own idea of society is impossible without a still larger assumption—not a few, but a whole nation of 'immaculate people.' In *Some Social Remedies* he rebukes this easy trick of making a scapegoat of the government, while the people themselves are professing 'a distortion of Christianity' which allows of orgies of brutal greed. Again, when he objects to the ideal of Socialism that people do not want it, the retort is obvious. 'None but the wise and pure can choose the wise and pure.' Very well; but the question is whether men who have a little wisdom and a little purity cannot choose other men who have a little more than they. The fact that they often fail to do so does not in any way justify us in declaring that they cannot. 'And if all men were wise and pure there would be no need of organisation.' This sentence cannot exactly express the author's thought. Who can imagine a state of society where organisation is not needed? There may, indeed, be people such as those against whom Tolstoy launches a special warning, 'modern Sadducees who, in the name of science and civilisation, aiming only at the continuation of the present state of things, assemble at meetings, write books and make speeches, promising to organise a good and peaceful life for people without their making any effort.' But there are also, as we know, men and women who conceive of society as an organised brotherhood in which the most important gains will be not material, but mental and moral. It is not enough to tell these people that governments are necessarily base, for they know that, in some countries at least, the people can at any time, if they will it, have a government that reflects the best things in their own minds. Not only is the objection to everything that can be represented as coercion carried to lengths which would render every kind of social union and every large social undertaking—say, the relief of famine or the transportation of the Dukhobortsi—

impossible, but ultimately the logic of anarchism breaks down in Tolstoy's own thought. In a paper in support of Henry George's land theory he says, 'Humanity advances continually towards the enlightenment of its consciousness, and to the institution of modes of life corresponding to this consciousness.' Just so. He instances the abolition of slavery (which would never have come about if the more enlightened social consciousness of the time had had no governmental organisation through which to act), and he goes on to declare that 'to-morrow committees might be appointed to examine and deliberate on his (Henry George's) scheme and its transformation into law.' And, as Mr. Aylmer Maude says,* 'Tolstoy himself does not profess to have ceased to use postage-stamps which are issued, or the highway that is maintained, by a government which collects taxes by force.'

These are the easy, the obvious, criticisms. A certain over-emphasis is characteristic of the prophetic mind. The fundamental truth remains, and men can only ignore it at their peril. In the measure in which it expresses force, and not cooperation or consent, government is an evil. That gives us a perfectly clear and a sufficiently high standard of judgment. True civilisation consists in the liberation of love from the bondage of outer authority. History is strewn with the dead bones

* *Tolstoy and His Problems*—a book of the utmost interest and value to the student.

of empires that depended on force; and if they persist in following their present paths the empires of Britain and Russia will follow those of Rome and Byzantium into oblivion. Religion and art are always worlds of real life because there, strong as convention and self-interest may be, the soul of man is always stronger and gaining strength. In western countries the belief in authoritative institutions has reached the last degree of infatuation. The evils of a bureaucratic system are patent enough, yet every little reform must needs be embodied in an Act of Parliament or a County Council bylaw and enforced through a new body of officials. The immediate money cost of internal government increases nearly as rapidly as that of foreign adventure; and the money cost is nothing beside the weakening of individual and social initiative. The belief in big businesses and big political machines has become a positive mania; only a man here and there dares to withstand it. The law stands over the individual as Mother Church once did—majestic, all-embracing, infallible; contempt of humanity is inculcated in a thousand forms; 'contempt of court' is a horrible offence. Unconvicted scoundrels flourish, and even claim our homage. But let the starving tramp intrude upon an absentee landlord's game preserve and he shall suffer. On the ground of armaments which it has itself supplied, Birmingham, greedy after more gold-mines, may make war upon a little State of old-fashioned farmers; but it is the duped country that must pay the piper. Add to these normal operations of unrestrained class power the hypnotic influence of the newspaper press, which holds the masses as the circus did in imperial Rome, the starving of the young mind in board schools, the degradation of the young body in factory towns, the corruption that prevails in commerce, the disappearance even of the ideal of a free, open life in touch with Nature, and how can any vagary of lunacy or crime surprise us? In this oppressive and hopeless emergency, when all the grand old voices of England are dead, it is to a small village in central Russia that we turn for a reminder of the simple truth.

Tolstoy has, then, lessons both for the individualist and the socialist. Most of the ordinary arguments against anarchism leave him untouched, because his appeal is not to individual right but to individual duty, not to self-advantage but to self-sacrifice. He is at the opposite pole from the Mr. Tucker of Boston whose maxim is that '"mind your own business" is the only moral law.' His political philosophy is, as I have said, a natural outcome of life in a country where the centrifugal impulse has been produced by bitter experience, and where agrarian communism, already partly realised, would be more easily extended than in any other European country. But, if in some important respects Russia is approaching our own position, in some others we are degenerating towards that of Russia. Another Russian thinker,

INTRODUCTION 41

Prince Kropotkin, in his striking work, entitled *Fields, Factories, and Workshops*, declares that the extreme division of labour that has made England what she is, is everywhere doomed, and that a contrary movement of decentralisation, which will gradually bring about an 'integrated variety' of occupations, industrial, agricultural, and intellectual, in each place, is now perceptible. Whether time vindicates this, or not, as a general forecast, it is now plain that the Socialist formula, 'the collective ownership of the means of production, distribution and exchange,' leaves untouched some vital questions on which the future of England depends. State-owned factories and mines might be preferable to factories and mines run for private profit, social trusts to private trusts; but the previous question rises more insistently in the minds of thinking men—Do we want, are we destined, to continue a nation of factory 'hands'; are the national trade and industry to remain substantially what they are to-day? Is this terrible London to continue growing larger and larger, fattening on its yearly tribute of country blood? Are Lancashire and the West Riding and the Black Country to be as they are to the end of the chapter? At any rate, machine slavery, the degradation of town life, the curse of over-specialisation, the iron doom of shop and office and factory employment, are hardly things which the clear-sighted reformer cares to take on trust or to treat with the gentle plasters of the Fabian Society. Socialism would have made better progress if it had not seemed to be wholly or primarily concerned with machinery and profits. Tolstoy is stimulating as much by his insistence upon the superior importance of moral over material progress as by his marvellous power of depicting the drama of the inner life. His attempt to formulate a moral dynamic is open to criticism, but it voices a hunger that is spreading and deepening in every country where machine industry and plutocracy are the governing conditions of the popular life. The comparative failure of purely economic Socialism confirms the impression that the people require the inspiration of a faith at once more Utopian and more actual. That the economic formula is so easy of acceptance—that it makes no present personal demand on the individual, that it has become as respectable as the creeds of the churches—is really a fatal obstacle. Men do not want an easy and respectable formula; they want a gospel which will really promise them release from their present servitude. Tolstoy's doctrine of bread-labour, his unbounded faith in the country life and country people, do at least point the way of escape from over-specialisation, from the slavery of the machine, and from the manifold evils of city life. A conception of the good life must, he insists, precede citizenship; a conception of the good State must precede its realisation. He belongs to that elder generation of humanists who never learned, and were never required, to specialise themselves down to the level of technical education boards, county council committees, and schools of economics. They stood—Emerson, Carlyle, Mazzini, Ruskin—for morals as a whole, and especially for the union of ethics and economics. They were nearer to the Declaration of Independence and the French Revolution, for one thing; liberty, equality, and fraternity always presented themselves to their minds as an inseparable tri-unity. The cult of the expert can offer us no substitute for a rounded conception of the ideal life and the ethics which that conception demands. It is absurd to suggest that the anti-State sentiment natural in Russia is equally proper here. But only those have a right to scoff at the principle of no-government who feel confident that a State which decent men may loyally support is attainable, and who are prepared to give their lives for its attainment. For the rest, Tolstoy's absorbing interest in the moral potentiality of the individual, in woman, in art, in the labourer, in the abolition of ruling castes, established hypocrisies, and prejudices and violence between nations, gives tremendous force to his appeal to thousands of men who cannot accept all his particular deductions.

The farcical excommunication reminds me that he has escaped martyrdom, so far, just because he is the one person in the empire whom the

Tsar himself dare not touch. That fact is eloquent testimony not only of his genius, which is universally admitted, but of the effectiveness and practicality of his teaching, which by foreign critics are very generally disputed. It is, indeed, one of the most remarkable spectacles in history, this immunity of the arch sedition-monger under the completest despotism of the time. Hardly a page that he has put forth in the last twenty years but has contained some scathing indictment of the falseness, the cruelty, of the social forms maintained by imperial authority around him. His contemporaries have to content themselves with indirect comments upon the diseases of public life, with veiled satire and allegorical fiction. He alone can say the plain truth without fear of the direst penalties; and surely the surgeon's knife was never used so unsparingly. What the censor forbids is secretly copied and passed from hand to hand throughout the empire, and more than one self-appointed missionary has suffered imprisonment for zeal in this direction.

He has founded no sect, no school larger than the little group of troubled peasants who gather for advice and assistance under the 'poor people's tree' at Yasnaya Polyana. A mere handful of men have followed the extreme lengths of his example in the renunciation of wealth, power, and luxury. It is only in spirit that his own household is united. He represents heaven, as P. A. Sergyenko puts it, while his wife, the excellent woman to whom the world owes so much, represents the earth. But it is the spirit of operative love, of unflinching sincerity and faithfulness to high ideals, not the particular application and precept, that is the essential thing. There is no need to exaggerate the material sacrifices which Leo Tolstoy has made. Actually he lives in assured comfort, though in perfect simplicity. In his seventy-third year he still rode the horse and the bicycle, played tennis, enjoyed music, romped with the children, and, in brief, showed himself, a sane, highly-vitalised personality, far removed from the narrowness of the eastern ascetic. It is this sanity and grip of real things that make his example so powerful, his spirit so infectious. In the record of the last decade in Europe, few finer episodes will be found than the aged writer's campaigns against famine, religious persecution, the flogging of peasants, and militarism. No other modern teacher has had to contend with such a desperate environment, and no other has succeeded in giving such an inspiring picture of love triumphant over the world. One cannot think of so very human a figure as, in the false old sense, a saint. He will not be canonised by any church; and it is only after long years of laborious growth into complete self-possession and self-expression that this rare mind shows us, reflected, all the agonising search and struggle of the soul of our time. As we glance back over the story of his life, theories, prescriptions, and discussions are forgotten, and we can think only with love and reverence of this modern patriarch, so lonely amid the daily-enlarging congregation of the hearts he has awakened to a sense of the mystery, the terror, the splendour and joy of human destinies.

G. H. PERRIS.

ACKNOWLEDGMENT

IN preparing the following extracts, I have received the most generous aid from Russian and English friends of Count Tolstoy, and from his translators and publishers. Mr. and Mrs. Aylmer Maude have given me franchise of their excellent translations, and Mr. Tchertkoff has extended this privilege to all the publications of the Free Age Press. I am also indebted to the house of Walter Scott, Limited, pioneers in publishing Tolstoy in English, for permission to quote from some of their translations, especially *What must We do, then?* and *The Kingdom of God is within You.* A few extracts are now translated for the first time, and a larger number have been specially rendered; for these I have to thank Mr. T. Rothstein and Mr. F. Volkhovsky. In the work of selection and compression, I have been helped by my brother, F. F. Perris.

It will, of course, be understood that I am solely responsible for the choice of passages—especially for the perhaps rather impertinent experiment of an autobiographical chapter—and for their abbreviation and arrangement. The great bulk of Tolstoy's writings and their richness of thought have made it, difficult to restrict this volume to its proper limits. For any obscurity or apparent inconsistency I am probably to blame; but a book like this is distinctly intended as an introduction to, not as a substitute for, the original writings.

CHAPTER I

AUTOBIOGRAPHICAL AND DESCRIPTIVE

I.—Youth

WHEN I try to recollect my mother as she was at that time, I am only able to picture to myself her brown eyes, with their invariable expression of kindness and love, the little mole on her neck just below the tiny curls, her embroidered white collar, and her delicate dry hand which so often caressed me and which I so often kissed. Her general expression, however, eludes me. . . . When mamma smiled, her face, always beautiful, became incomparably more beautiful, and everything around grew, as it were, brighter and more cheerful. If during the trying hours of life I could but catch a glimpse of that smile, I should never know what sorrow means. It seems to me that it is only the smile that constitutes what is called the beauty of a face: if the smile adds to the charm of the face, the latter is beautiful; if it does not change it, it is common; if it spoils it, it is ugly.

The harvest was at its height. The immense shimmering yellow field was closed on one side by a high bluish forest, which at that time seemed to me the most distant and mysterious place on earth, beyond which either the world came to an end or there extended uninhabited lands. The field was covered by sheaves and people. In the tall thick rye one could see, here and there, on some cleared strip, the bent back of a harvest woman, the ears of corn swinging as she took them between her fingers, and the figure of a woman in the shade, bending over a cradle. . . . The hum of human voices, the stamping of horses' hoofs and the sound of cart-wheels, the gay whistling of the quails, the buzzing of insects that hovered about in the air in close masses, the smell of wormwood and straw and the horses' steaming flanks, the thousands of various tints and shades cast by the burning sun over the bright yellow field and the blue distance of the forest and the lily-white clouds, the white air-threads flying about or settling on the fields—all this I saw, heard, and felt.

The windows, which looked out to the forest, were lit up by the moon, which was almost full. The long white figure of the crazy fanatic was illuminated, on one side, by the pale silvery rays, and was, on the other, enveloped in a black shadow which, together with that of the window-frames, fell on the floor and on the walls, reaching up to the ceiling. The watchman in the yard was striking his brazen board. His enormous arms crossed on his heart, his head bent, sighing deeply and incessantly, Grisha stood silently before the holy images, and then heavily knelt and began to pray. At first he softly said some prayers, emphasising only a few of the words. Then he repeated them, but in a louder voice and with greater animation. He began to utter words of his own, trying with marked difficulty to express himself in Slavonic. His words were incoherent, but touching. He prayed for all his benefactors (by these he meant all who gave him shelter)—amongst others, for mother and for us; he prayed for himself, asking

God to forgive him his great sins, and repeating: 'Oh, Lord, forgive my enemies.' Groaning, he now raised himself; and then, saying over and over again the same words, prostrated himself on the floor; and then once more raised himself, in spite of the heavy irons that made a dry and sharp sound when knocking against the floor. Volodya gave me a sharp pinch in the leg; but I did not even turn round—only rubbed the place with my hand and still followed all the movements and words of Grisha with a feeling of childish surprise, pity, and awe. Instead of the fun and the laughter which I anticipated when entering the lumber-room, I felt a nervous shiver passing through my body, my heart sinking within me. . . . Plenty of water has flowed since then, many memories of the past have lost their importance to me and become hazy dreams, even Grisha, the wanderer, has long since come to the end of his pilgrimages; but the impression he made on me, and the feelings which he evoked within me, will never die out of my memory.

The requiem came to an end, the face of the deceased was uncovered, and all present, with the exception of ourselves, approached the coffin one by one and kissed the dead. One of the last to come to pay the last honours was a peasant woman, holding in her arms a pretty girl about five years of age, whom she had brought with her, goodness knows for what purpose. At that moment I dropped my wet handkerchief on the floor and was going to pick it up; but no sooner did I stoop to do so than I was startled by a terrific piercing scream full of such horror that, were I even to live a hundred years, I shall never be able to forget it. Whenever I think of it, a cold shiver passes through my body. I raised my head: on the footstool, by the side of the coffin, there stood the same peasant woman, struggling to hold the child, which, waving her little arms, her frightened face thrown back and her wide eyes fixed on the face of the deceased, was wildly, furiously screaming. I uttered a cry which was, I think, still more frightful than the one which had just startled me, and ran out of the room. It was only then that I understood whence the strong and heavy smell came which filled the room together with the odour of the incense: and the thought that the face which but a few days ago was full of beauty and gentleness, the face of one whom I loved more than anything else in the world, could inspire such a horror revealed to me for the first time, as it were, the bitter truth, and filled my soul with despair.

In the vestibule the *samovar* is boiling already, and Mitka, the postilion, red as a lobster, blows it with all his might. Outside, it is damp and misty; something like steam rises from the odorous dunghill. The sun illuminates brightly and cheerfully the eastern part of the sky, as well as the dew-covered and glittering straw roofs of the sheds which border the yard. Under the sheds one sees the horses tied to their mangers and hears their measured chewing. A shaggy little dog, which has coiled itself up on the dry dunghill just before sunrise, lazily stretches itself, and, wagging its tail, trots off to another part of the yard. The busy housewife throws open the creaking gate, drives the dreamy cows into the street, where one could already hear the stamping, the lowing, and the bleating of the herd, and exchanges a few words with the sleepy neighbour. Philip, with his shirt-sleeves turned up, draws a bucket from the deep well by means of a wheel, splashing the clear water, and empties it into an oaken trough, near which a number of ducks, already aroused from their sleep, splash about in a pool. I watch with pleasure the dignified face of Philip with its large and bushy beard, and the thick veins and muscles that stand out sharply on his bare and powerful arms whenever he makes an effort.

There, on the footpath, which winds near the high road, we see a number of slowly moving figures. These are pilgrim-women. Their heads are muffled in dirty handkerchiefs, on their backs are birch-bark baskets, their feet are wrapped up in dirty, torn rags, and clad in heavy bast shoes. Rhythmically swinging their sticks, and scarcely looking at us, they slowly and heavily proceed one after the other, and different questions rise in my mind: Whither are they going? What for? When will the long shadows which they cast on the road join the shadows of the cytisus which they will have to pass by?

Suddenly the entire country around changes its aspect and falls into a gloom. A tremor passes through the aspen woods; the leaves assume a turbid whitish tint, forming a striking contrast with the lilac background of the storm-cloud, and rustle and twirl about. The tops of the big birch trees begin to swing, and bundles of dry grass are blown over the road. Martins and white-breasted swallows hover round our coach, as if with the intention of stopping us, and pass under the very breasts of our horses. Jackdaws with dishevelled wings fly somewhat sideways along the wind. The edges of the leathern apron, with which we have buttoned ourselves up, begin to rise, letting through gusts of damp wind, and, fluttering to and fro, knock against the frame of the coach. Suddenly a flash of lightning, in the very coach as it were, blinds our eyes and illuminates for a moment the grey cloth, the galloons, and the figure of Volodya coiled up in the corner. Simultaneously a majestic peal of thunder rolls over our very heads, and then, ascending, as it were, higher and higher and sweeping in an ever wider and wider spiral, gradually gains force and finally ends with a deafening crash that makes one involuntarily tremble and hold one's breath. The wrath of God! what poesy in that popular idea! . . . 'Little father! help a poor man, for Christ's sake!' sounds a weak voice, and the beggar crosses himself and bows low at every word. I cannot express the feeling of cold horror that seized my soul at this moment. My hair was trembling with fear, and my eyes were fixed and stupidly gazing at the beggar. . . . A dazzling flash, suddenly filling the gorge with a fiery light, compels the horses to stop. It is accompanied, without the least interval, by such a deafening crash of thunder that the entire vault of heaven seems to fall upon our heads. The wind grows stronger; the manes and tails of the horses, Vassily's cloak and the edges of the apron fly in the same direction and flutter desperately in the furious gusts of the wind. A heavy rain-drop falls upon the leathern top of the coach, another, a third, a fourth; and all at once we hear the rolling of a drum, as it were, and the country around begins to resound with the measured noise of the falling rain. I can see by the movements of Vassily's elbows that he is unfastening the purse; the beggar, still crossing himself and bowing, runs close to the very wheels, making one tremble lest he should fall under them. 'Give me something, for Christ's sake!' At last a copper coin flashes through the air, and the poor wretch, in wet rags that tightly cling to his lean limbs, stops in the middle of the road with a puzzled expression on his face and, tottering from the wind, disappears from sight. . . . Now the rain grows less. The storm-cloud begins to break up into curly plumes. It brightens up where the sun must be, and through its greyish-white edges one can catch a glimpse of the clear blue sky. Another moment, and a timid sunbeam is playing already on the pools on the road, on the sheets of the fine, perpendicular rain falling as through a sieve, and on the cleanly washed and shining green of the grass by the roadside.

'We shall not always live together, you know,' said Katenka. . . . 'You are rich, and we are poor. . . .' These words and the ideas conveyed by them appeared to me uncommonly strange. . . . Still I understood that it would not do to speak with Katenka about it, and a sort of a practical instinct, so to say, in opposition to the logical reasoning, told me that she was right, and that it would be out of place to explain to her my thoughts. . . . For the first time the idea clearly presented itself to my mind that not we alone (that is, our family) live in the world, that not all interests concentrate upon us, but that there is another life of other people who have nothing in common with us, who do not care about us, who even have no idea of our existence. Undoubtedly, I knew all this before, but I knew it not as I grasped it now. I did not realise it, I did not feel it. . . . With our arrival in Moscow the change in my view of things and persons and my attitude towards them became still more marked.

During the year in which I lived a secluded, self-concentrated, and moral life, all the abstract questions about the destiny of man, future life, or immortality of the soul, were already arising in my brain, and my feeble youthful mind was trying with all the passion of inexperience to solve those problems, the appreciation of which constitutes the highest point attainable by the human mind, but which no one can solve. . . . It appeared to me at one time that happiness does not depend on external causes, but on our attitude towards them, that a person who can bear pain can never be unhappy. And so, in order to get used to pain, I would, for five minutes at a time, hold Tatischeff's Dictionaries in my outstretched hands, or go to the scullery and there beat myself on the bare back with a rope till tears involuntarily came to my eyes. Another time, on recollecting suddenly that death may come to me at any hour, at any moment, I decided—wondering how it was that people had not grasped it up till now—that man cannot be happy otherwise than by enjoying the present and ignoring the future; and for three consecutive days, under the influence of this thought, I did not do my lessons, but simply lay on my bed, reading a novel and eating cake with honey, bought with my last pence. But by no philosophical system was I carried away to such an extent as by scepticism, which at one time nearly brought me to the verge of madness. I imagined that there was nobody and nothing in the world but myself, that the objects around are not objects, but images which only appear when one thinks of them, and disappear as soon as one leaves off thinking of them. In a word, I agreed with Schelling that what exists is not things, but solely one's attitude towards them. There were moments when, under the influence of this fixed idea, I attained such heights of folly that I would suddenly turn round to see whether I could not find a vacuum where I was not. What a miserable, insignificant spring of moral activity the human mind is! My feeble brain could not penetrate the impenetrable, but instead was losing in its fruitless efforts one moral conviction after the other—things that for the sake of happiness in my life I should never have touched. From all this heavy moral toil I did not derive anything but a superfine flexibility of mind that unloosened my strength of will, and a habit, a predilection for constant moral analysis that destroyed the freshness of my feelings and the lucidity of my reason. . . . I was simply losing my wits.

I involuntarily long to cross as quickly as possible the desert of my adolescence, and to reach that happy time when again the truly delicate and noble feeling of friendship illuminated the close of that period and began a new one full of charm and poesy—that of youth. . . . Under the influence of Nekhlyudov I involuntarily adopted his views, the essential part of which was the enthusiastic adoration of the ideal of virtue and a belief in the destiny of man to progress continually towards perfection. At that time it seemed a very easy thing to improve man morally, to extirpate all vice and misfortunes of mankind; it seemed so simple to improve oneself, to learn all virtue and to be happy. . . . However, God alone knows whether these noble, youthful dreams were really so ridiculous, and whose fault it is that they were not realised.

I became this summer more intimate than ever before with our young ladies on account of the passion for music that had suddenly awakened within me. . . . I at once began playing *salon* pieces, and played them, of course, with feeling—*avec âme*—as Katenka herself acknowledged, without the least notion of time. The choice of pieces was the usual one—waltzes, galops, sentimental songs, arrangements for the pianoforte—all those things by lovely composers which anyone with a grain of common sense will pick out in a music-shop from a heap of excellent things and say: 'These are the things which you must not play. Nothing worse, more tasteless and insipid has ever been put on music paper. . . .' Notwithstanding this muddle and hypocrisy, there was, however, so far as I can recollect, some talent in me, as music often impressed me till tears flowed from my eyes, and the things which I loved, I could, without notes, make out on the piano myself. Possibly, had somebody taught me to regard music as an end in itself, as a pleasure for itself, not as a means to evoke ladies' applause by the quickness and the sentimentality of the performance, I might have, indeed, become a good musician.

Another occupation of mine during that summer was the reading of French novels, of which Volodya had brought a good number. . . . I would find in myself all the passions painted in these novels and a likeness with all the characters—the heroes as well as the villains—just as a morbid-minded person finds in himself the symptoms of all possible diseases when reading a medical book. . . . Thanks to those novels I even formed new ideals of moral qualities which I wanted to attain. First of all I wanted, in all my actions and conduct, to be *noble* ; . . . then to be *passionate*, and lastly—what I was inclined to even before—to be *comme il faut*. . . . This latter notion was in my life one of the most pernicious and false inculcated in me by education and society. . . . My *comme il faut* consisted, first and foremost, in speaking excellent

French and, especially, in pronouncing it faultlessly. The second condition of *comme il faut* was to have long nails, clean and polished; the third, to be able to make a graceful bow, to dance and to carry on a conversation; the fourth—and very important, too—to be indifferent to everything, and to wear a constant expression of elegant, contemptuous weariness. The relation of the boots to the trousers of a man at once decided in my eyes his station in life. ... It is awful to think what an amount of the best time in my youth I have wasted on the acquirement of this quality. ...

The spree was at its height. I had had already a glassful of hot punch, another was filled for me, my temples were throbbing, the flame seemed red as fire, everybody around was shouting and laughing; and still not only did it not seem merry, but I was even certain that both I and the rest felt bored, though, for some mysterious reason, we thought it necessary to pretend to be happy.... I remember that besides the same feeling of lack of control in all my limbs which I experienced during the dinner at Yar's, I had on that night such a severe headache that I was awfully afraid lest I should drop down dead on the spot. I also remember that we, goodness knows for what purpose, sat down on the floor, and, moving our arms in imitation of rowing, sang: 'Down the mother Volga,' I myself thinking all the time that it was stupid to do all this. I further remember that, lying on the floor and hardly being able to move about the legs, I wrestled in the gipsy style, nearly broke somebody's neck, and thought that this would not have happened had he not been drunk. I remember also that we had some supper and drank something else, that I went for a moment outside to catch a breath of fresh air, and my head was cold; and when going home I noticed that it was awfully dark, that the step of the carriage became slanting and slippery, and that it was impossible to lean on Kuzma, as he was very weak and bent like a rag. Most of all, I remember that all through that night I continually felt that I was acting very foolishly. Each of us considered it his duty to pretend to be jolly in order not to spoil the general merry-making. Besides, strange to say, I felt it incumbent on me to feign this, if only for the reason that the bowl contained three bottles of champagne at ten roubles each, and ten bottles of rum, four roubles each, which altogether made a total of seventy roubles, besides the supper.—*Childhood, Boyhood, and Youth.*

I was christened and educated in the faith of the Orthodox Greek Church; I was taught it in my childhood, and I learned it in my youth. Nevertheless, at eighteen years of age, when I quitted the university, I had discarded all belief in everything that I had been taught. To judge by what I can now remember, I could never have had a very serious belief; it must have been a kind of trust in this teaching based on a trust in my teachers and elders, and a trust, moreover, not very firmly grounded. I remember once, in my twelfth year, a boy, now long since dead, Vladimir M——, a pupil in a gymnasium, spent a Sunday with us, and brought us the news of the last discovery in the gymnasium, namely, that there was no God, and that all we were taught on the subject was a mere invention. This was in 1838. I remember well how interested my elder brothers were in this news. I sympathised then with the jokes of my elders, and drew from them this conclusion: that I was bound to learn my catechism, and go to church, but that it was not necessary to think of my religious duties more seriously. I also remember that I read Voltaire when I was very young, and that his tone of mockery amused without disgusting me. The gradual estrangement from all belief went on in me, as it does, and always has done, in those of the same social position and culture.

The belief instilled from childhood gradually disappeared in me, as in so many others, but with this difference, that I was conscious of my own disbelief. At fifteen years of age I had begun to read philosophical works. From the age of sixteen I ceased to pray, and ceased also, from conviction, to attend the services of the Church, and to fast. I no longer accepted the faith of my childhood, but I had a vague belief in *something*, though I do not think I could exactly explain what. Now, when I think over that time, I see clearly that all the faith I had, the only belief which, apart from mere animal instinct, swayed my life, was a belief in a possibility of perfection, though what it was in itself, or what would be its results, I was unable to say. At first, of course, moral perfection seemed to me the main end, but I soon found myself contemplating in its stead an ideal of general perfectibility; in other words, I wished to be better, not in my own eyes, nor in those of God, but in the sight of other men. This feeling again soon ended in another—the desire to have more power than others, to secure for myself a greater share of fame, of social distinction, and of wealth.

I honestly desired to make myself a good and virtuous man; but I was young, I had passions, and I stood alone, altogether alone, in my search after virtue. Every time I tried to express the longings of my heart for a truly virtuous life, I was met with contempt and derisive laughter, but directly I gave way to the lowest of my passions, I was praised and encouraged. I found ambition, love of power, love of gain, lechery, pride, anger, vengeance, held in high esteem. I gave way to these passions, and becoming like unto my elders, felt that the place which I filled in the world satisfied those around me. My kind-hearted aunt, a really good woman, used to say to me that there was one thing above all others which she wished for me—an intrigue with a married woman : '*Rien ne forme un jeune homme comme une liaison avec une femme comme il faut.*' Another of her wishes for my happiness was that I should become an adjutant, and, if possible, to the Emperor. The greatest happiness of all for me she thought would be that I should find a wealthy bride, who would bring me as her dowry an enormous number of serfs.—*My Confession.*

II.—Soldier, Landlord, Artist

Prince Nekhlyudov was nineteen years of age when he, a university graduate of the third term, visited his landed estates during the summer holidays and remained there all through the summer alone. In the autumn he wrote to his aunt a letter in his irregular boyish hand :—

'I have made up my mind to a thing on which the entire course of my life depends. I am leaving the university in order to devote myself to country life, for which I feel I was born. . . . I found affairs there in an indescribable muddle. Being desirous of putting them in order, and having closely investigated them, I discovered that the root of the evil lies in the wretched, poverty-stricken condition of the peasants—a thing that can only be remedied by long labour and patience. . . . Is it not my sacred and immediate duty to take care of the seven hundred human souls for whose welfare I shall have to answer before God? Is it not a sin to leave them to the mercy of the rude elders and managers for the sake simply of pleasure or ambition? . . . I feel myself quite capable of being a good landowner, and there is no need, in order to become such a one (as I understand the word), to have a university degree or a title such as you desire for me. . . .'

'My God, my God!' thought Nekhlyudov, . . . 'were my dreams of the aim and duties of my life nothing but empty words? Why do I feel so heavy and dissatisfied, when, I had thought that, once I discovered this road, I should always experience the same fulness of satisfaction as at the time when these thoughts first dawned on my mind? . . . .' With all the charm of the unknown, his youthful imagination pictured to him the voluptuous figure of a woman, and he thought: that is it, the unexpressed desire. But another, a higher feeling whispered to him: it is *not* that, and made him look for something else. Again, his inexperienced, ardent mind, ascending ever higher and higher into the sphere of abstraction, discovered, as it seemed to him, the laws of the universe, and he with a proud pleasure dwelt on these thoughts. But once more a higher feeling whispered to him: it is *not* that, and made him seek again, and again feel uneasy. Without thoughts or desires, as always happens after intense mental activity, he lay down on his back under a tree and began contemplating the translucent morning clouds that glided over him across the deep and limitless sky. . . . 'Love, self-sacrifice—this is the only true happiness, not subject to accident,' he repeated, smiling and waving his hands. Applying this thought in every direction of life, and finding it confirmed both in life and in that inner voice which whispered to him: it is *that*, he experienced a novel sensation of joy and ecstasy. 'And so I must do good in order to be happy,' he thought, and his entire future vividly presented itself before his mind not in abstractions, as before, but in concrete forms of the life of a landowner. 'He saw before him, as it were, an immense field, the life which he would devote to good, and in which, therefore, he would be happy. He need not look for a sphere of activity—he had one ready for him; he had direct duties—he owned peasants. ... What a joyous and fruitful work there lay before him! 'To influence this simple, receptive, uncorrupted people, to free them from poverty, to give them contentedness, to pass to the peasants the education which I, fortunately, possess, to correct their vices, born of ignorance and superstition, to develop their morality, to make them love the Good. ... What a brilliant, happy future! ... I and my wife, whom I love as no one has ever loved anybody before, will live always amidst these quiet, poetical, rural surroundings, with our children and, perhaps, with our old aunt. We have our mutual love, our love to our children, and we both know that our aim and destiny in life is the good. ...' 'Where are those dreams?' the young man was now asking himself as he neared the house after his visits; 'for more than a year I have been seeking happiness on this road, and what have I found? True, sometimes I do feel that I can be content; but it is such a dry, rational contentment! No, I am simply dissatisfied with myself! ... Aunt was right when she wrote that it is easier to find happiness for oneself than to give it to others. Have

my peasants become richer? Have they become better educated or more moral? Not in the least! They are no happier, whilst I am getting more and more unhappy with every day. If I could but see progress in my undertaking! if I could but see gratitude! ... No, I see only false routine, vice, mistrust, helplessness. I am spending the best years of my life in vain. ...'
And suddenly, as vividly as that country walk through the forest and his dreams of a landowner's life had risen in his mind before—just as vividly he now saw mentally his student's room at Moscow, where he sat late into the night before a solitary candle, together with his fellow-student and dear friend. Then the future was full of pleasure, of every kind of activity, of glitter, of success, and led them both undoubtedly to what they then conceived to be the supreme good in the world —to fame. ... But at this moment he was already nearing the steps of his house, where about a score peasants of the village and manor were standing and waiting for his arrival with various requests, and he had to turn from his dreams to reality. ... ' He listened to all the requests and complaints, and, having advised some, settled the complaint of others and given his promises to the third, he entered his room with a mixed feeling of weariness, shame, helplessness and penitence.
—*A Russian Proprietor.*

Disenchantment certainly awaits you if you are entering Sevastopol for the first time. ...

You enter the great Hall of Assembly. You have but just opened the door when the sight and smell of forty or fifty seriously wounded men and of those who have undergone amputation—some in hammocks, the majority upon the floor—suddenly strike you. Trust not to the feeling which detains you upon the threshold of the hall; be not ashamed of having come to *look at* the sufferers, be not ashamed to approach and address them: the unfortunates like to see a sympathising human face, they like to tell of their sufferings and to hear words of love and interest. . . . Now, if your nerves are strong, pass through the door on the left. In yonder room they are applying bandages and performing operations. There you will see doctors with their arms bloodstained above the elbow, and with pale, stern faces, busied about a cot upon which, with eyes widely opened, and uttering, as in delirium, incoherent, sometimes simple and touching words, lies a wounded man under the influence of chloroform. The doctors are busy with the repulsive but beneficent work of amputation. You see the sharp, curved knife enter the healthy, white body, you see the wounded man suddenly regain consciousness with a piercing cry and curses, you see the army surgeon fling the amputated arm into a corner, you see another wounded man, lying in a litter in the same apartment, shrink convulsively and groan as he gazes at the operation upon his comrade, not so much from physical pain as from the moral torture of anticipation. You behold the frightful, soul-stirring scenes; you behold war, not from its conventional, beautiful, and brilliant side, with music and drum-beat, with fluttering flags and galloping generals, but you behold war in its real aspect—in blood, in suffering, in death. On emerging from this house of pain, you will infallibly experience a sensation of pleasure. . . . The sight of the clear sky, the brilliant sun, the fine city, the open church, and the soldiers moving about in various directions soon restores your mind to its normal condition of frivolity, petty cares, and absorption in the present alone.

Hundreds of bodies, freshly smeared with blood, of men who two hours previous had been filled with divers lofty or petty hopes and desires, now lay, with stiffened limbs, in the dewy, flowery valley which separated the bastion from the trench, and on the level floor of the chapel for the dead in Sevastopol; hundreds of men crawled, twisted, and groaned, with curses and prayers on their parched lips, some amid the corpses in the flower-strewn vale, others on stretchers, on cots, and on the bloodstained floor of the hospital. And still, as on the days preceding, the dawn glowed over Sapun Mountain, the twinkling stars paled, the white mist spread abroad from the dark sounding sea, the red glow illuminated the east, long crimson cloudlets darted across the blue horizon; and still, as on days preceding, the powerful, all-beautiful sun rose up, giving promise of joy, love, and happiness to all who dwell in the world.

Who is the villain of this sketch, who is the hero? All are good, and all are evil. Neither Kalugin, with his brilliant bravery—*bravoure de gentilhomme*—and his vanity, the instigator of all his deeds; nor Praskukhin, the empty-headed, harmless man, though he fell in battle for the faith, the throne, and his native land; nor Mikhailoff, with his shyness; nor Pesth, a child with no firm convictions or principles, can be either the heroes or the villains of the tale. The hero of my tale, whom I love with all the strength of my soul, whom I have tried to set forth in all his beauty, and who has always been, is, and always will be, most beautiful, is—the truth.—*Sevastopol Sketches.*

I cannot now recall those years without a painful feeling of horror and loathing. I put men to death in war, I fought duels to slay others, I lost at cards, wasted the substance wrung from the sweat of peasants, punished the latter cruelly, rioted with loose women, and deceived men. Lying, robbery, adultery of all kinds, drunkenness, violence, and murder, all committed by me, not one crime omitted, and yet I was not the less considered by my equals a comparatively moral man. Such was my life during ten years.

During that time I began to write, out of vanity, love of gain, and pride. I followed as a writer the same path which I had chosen as a man. In order to obtain the fame and the money for which I wrote, I was obliged to hide what was good and bow down before what was evil. How often while writing have I cudgelled my brains to conceal under the mask of indifference or pleasantry those yearnings for something better which formed the real problem of my life! I succeeded in my object, and was praised.

At twenty-six years of age, on the close of the war, I came to St. Petersburg and made the acquaintance of the authors of the day. I met with a hearty reception and much flattery. Before I had time to look around, the prejudices and views of life common to the writers of the class with which I associated became my own, and completely put an end to all my former struggles after a better life. These views, under the influence of the dissipation into which I plunged, issued in a theory of life which justified it. The view taken by my fellow-writers was that life is development, and the principal part in that development is played by ourselves, the thinkers, while among the thinkers the chief influence is again due to ourselves, the poets. Our vocation is to teach mankind.

I was myself considered a marvellous *littérateur* and poet, and I therefore very naturally adopted this theory. Meanwhile, thinker and poet though I was, I wrote and taught I knew not what. For doing this I received large sums of money; I kept a splendid table, had an excellent lodging, associated with loose women, and received my friends handsomely; moreover, I had fame. It would seem, then, that what I taught must have been good; the faith in poetry and the development of life was a true faith, and I was one of its high priests, a post of great importance, and of profit. I long remained in this belief, and, at first, never once doubted its truth.

In the second, however, and especially in the third year of this way of life, I began to doubt the infallibility of the doctrine, and to examine it more closely. . . . When I doubted this faith in the influence of literary men, I began to examine more closely into the character and conduct of its chief professors, and I convinced myself that they were men who led immoral lives, most of them worthless and insignificant individuals, and far beneath the moral level of those with whom I had associated during my former dissipated and military career; these men, however, had none the less an amount of self-confidence only to be expected in those who are conscious of being saints, or in those for whom holiness is an empty name.

I grew disgusted with mankind and with myself, and discovered that this belief which I had accepted was a delusion. The strangest thing in all this was that, though I soon saw the falseness of the belief and renounced it, I did not renounce the position I had gained by it; I still called myself a thinker, a poet, and a teacher. I was simple enough to imagine that I, the poet and thinker, was able to teach other men without knowing myself what it was I attempted to teach. I had only gained a new vice by my companionship; it had developed pride in me to a morbid extreme, and my self-confidence in teaching what I did not know amounted almost to insanity.

I lived in this senseless manner another six years, up to the time of my marriage. During the interval I had been abroad. My life in Europe, and my acquaintance with many eminent and learned foreigners, confirmed my belief in the doctrine of general perfectibility, as I found the same theory prevailed among them. This belief took the form which is common among most cultivated men of the day. It may be summed up in the word 'progress.' . . . It was only at rare intervals that my feelings, and not my reason, were roused against the common superstition of our age, which leads men to ignore their own ignorance of life. Thus, during my stay in Paris, the sight of a public execution revealed to me the weakness of my superstitious belief in progress. When I saw the head divided from the body, and heard the sound with which they fell separately into the box, I understood, not with my reason, but with my whole being, that no theory of the wisdom of all established things, nor of progress, could justify such an act; and that if all the men in the world from the day of creation, by whatever theory, had found this thing necessary, it was not so—it was a bad thing—and that therefore I must judge of what was right and necessary, not by what men said and did, not by progress, but what I felt to be true in my heart. Another instance of the insufficiency of this superstition of progress as a rule for life occurred with the death of my brother. He fell ill while still young, suffered much during a whole year, and died in great pain. He was a man of great abilities, of a kind heart, and of a serious temper, but he died without understanding why he had lived, or what his death meant for him. No theories could give an answer to these questions either to him or to me, during the whole period of his long and painful lingering.

* On my return from abroad I settled in the country, and occupied myself with the organisation of schools for the peasantry. This occupation was especially grateful to me because it was free from the spirit of falseness so evident to me in the career of a literary teacher. Here again I acted in the name of progress, but this time I brought a spirit of critical inquiry to the system on which the progress rested. I said to myself that progress was often attempted in an irrational manner, and that it was necessary to leave a primitive people and the children of peasants perfectly free to choose the way of progress which they thought best. In reality I was still bent on the solution of the same impossible problem, how to teach without knowing what I had to teach. . . . It seems now absurd when I remember the experiments by which I carried out this whim of mine to teach, though I knew in my heart that I could teach nothing useful, because I myself did not know what was necessary.

After a year spent in this employment with the schools, I again went abroad, for the purpose of finding out how to teach under these conditions. I believed that I had found a solution abroad, and, armed with that conviction, I returned to Russia, the same year in which the peasants were freed from serfdom, and accepting the office of a country magistrate or arbitrator, I began to teach the uneducated people in the schools, and the educated classes in the journals which I published. Things seemed to be going on well, but I felt that my mind was not in a normal state, and that a change was near. I might then, perhaps, have come to that state of absolute despair to which I was brought fifteen years later, if it had not been for a new experience in life which promised me safety—the home life of a family man. For a year I occupied myself with my duties as arbitrator, with the schools, and my newspaper, and got so involved that I was harassed to death; my arbitration was one continual struggle, what to do in the schools became less and less clear, and my newspaper shuffling more and more repugnant to me. Always the same thing: trying to teach without knowing how or what. So that I fell ill, more with a mental than physical sickness, gave up everything, and started for the steppes to breathe a fresher air, to drink mare's milk, and live a mere animal life.

Soon after my return I married. The new circumstances of a happy family life by which I was now surrounded completely led my mind away from the search after the meaning of life as a whole. My life was concentrated in my family, my wife, and children, and, consequently, in the care for increasing the means of supporting them. The effort to attain individual perfection, already replaced by the striving after general progress, was again changed into an effort to secure the particular happiness of my family.

In this way fifteen years passed. Notwithstanding that during these fifteen years I looked upon the craft of authorship as a very trifling thing, I continued all the time to write. I had experienced the seductions of authorship, the temptations of an enormous pecuniary reward and of great applause for valueless work, and gave myself up to it as a means of improving my material position, and of stifling all the feelings which led me to my own life and that of society for the meaning in them. In my writings I taught what for me was the only truth—that the object of life should be our own happiness and that of our family.—*My Confession.*

III.—CONVERSION

By this rule I lived; but five years ago (1874) a strange state of mind-torpor began at times to grow upon me. I had moments of perplexity, of a stoppage, as it were, of life, as if I did not know how I was to live, what I was to do. I began to wander, and was a victim to low spirits. This, however, passed, and I continued to live as before. Later, these periods of perplexity grew more and more frequent, and invariably took the same form. During their continuance the same questions always presented themselves to me: 'Why?' and 'What after?' .. . . I became aware that this was not a mere passing phase of mental ill-health, but that the symptoms were of the utmost importance, and that if these questions continued to recur I must find an answer to them.

My life had come to a sudden stop. I was able to breathe, to eat, to drink, to sleep. I could not, indeed, help doing so; but there was no real life in me. I had not a single wish to strive for the fulfilment of what I could feel to be reasonable. The truth lay in this, that life had no meaning for me. Thus I, a healthy and a happy man, was brought to feel that I could live no longer, that an irresistible force was dragging me down into the grave. The idea of suicide came as naturally to me as formerly that of bettering my life. It had so much attraction for me that I was compelled to practise a species of self-deception in order to avoid carrying it out too hastily. I was unwilling to act hastily, only because I had determined first to clear away the confusion of my thoughts, and, that once done, I could always kill myself. I was happy, yet I hid away a cord to avoid being tempted to hang myself by it to one of the pegs between the cupboards of my study, where I undressed alone every evening. And I ceased to carry a gun because it offered too easy a way of getting rid of life. I knew not what I wanted; I was afraid of life; I shrank from it; and yet there *was* something I hoped for from it.

Such was the condition I had come to at a time when all the circumstances of my life were pre-eminently happy ones, and when I had not reached my fiftieth year. I had a good, a loving, and a well-beloved wife, good children, a fine estate, which, without much trouble on my part, continually increased my income; I was more than ever respected by my friends and acquaintances; I was praised by strangers, and could lay claim to having made my name famous without much self-deception. Moreover, my mind was neither deranged nor weakened; on the contrary, I enjoyed a mental and physical strength which I have seldom found in men of my class and pursuits; I could keep up with a peasant in mowing, and could continue mental labour for ten hours at a stretch without any evil consequences.

The mental state in which I then was seemed to me summed up in the following: My life was a foolish and wicked joke played upon me by I knew not whom. Notwithstanding my rejection of the idea of a Creator, that of a being who thus wickedly and foolishly made a joke of me seemed to me the most natural of all conclusions and the one that threw the most light upon my darkness. . . . Illness and death would come—indeed they had come—if not to-day, then to-morrow, to those whom I loved, to myself, and nothing would remain but stench and worms. All my acts, whatever I did, would sooner or later be forgotten, and I myself be nowhere. Why, then, busy oneself with anything?

However I may reason with myself that I cannot understand the meaning of life, that I must live without thinking, I cannot again begin to do so; I have done so too long already. I cannot now help seeing that each day and each night, as it passes, brings me nearer to death. I can see but this, because this alone is true—all the rest is a lie. . . . I felt a horror of what awaited me; I knew that this horror was more terrible than the position itself, but I could not patiently await the end. However persuasive the argument might be, that in any case something in the heart or elsewhere would burst and all be over, still I could not patiently await the end. The horror of the darkness was too great to bear, and I longed to free myself from it by a rope or a pistol ball. This was the feeling that, above all, drew me to think of suicide.

I sought an explanation of the questions which tormented me in every branch of human knowledge.

I sought that explanation painfully and long, not out of mere curiosity nor apathetically, but obstinately day and night. I sought it as a perishing man seeks safety, and I found nothing. I sought in all directions, and, thanks to a life of study, and also to the footing which I had gained in learned society, all the sources of knowledge were open to me, not merely through books, but through personal intercourse. I had the advantage of all that learning could answer to the question, 'What is life?' . . . I said to myself, 'I know now all that science so obstinately seeks to learn; but an answer to my question as to the meaning of my life is not to be obtained from science.' I saw that philosophy, notwithstanding, or perhaps because, an answer to my question had become the direct object of its inquiries, gave no answer but the one I had given to myself. 'What is the meaning of my life? It has none. Or, what will come of my life? Nothing. Or, why does all that is exist, and why do I exist? Because it does exist.' Thus my wanderings over the fields of knowledge not only failed to cure me of my despair, but increased it. One branch of knowledge gave no answer at all to the problem of life, another gave a direct answer which confirmed my despair and showed that the state to which I had come was not the result of my going astray, of any mental disorder, but, on the contrary, of my thinking rightly, of my being in agreement with the conclusions of the most powerful intellects among mankind.

Having failed to find an explanation in knowledge, I began to seek it in life itself, hoping to find it in the men who surrounded me; and I began to watch men like myself, to observe how they lived, and how they practically treated the question which had brought me

CONVERSION 77

to despair. I found that for those who occupied the same social position as myself there were four means of escape from the terrible state in which we all were. The first means of escape is Ignorance. It consists in not perceiving and understanding that life is an evil and an absurdity. . . . The second means of escape is the Epicurean. It consists in taking advantage of every good there is in life, while we know its hopelessness. . . . The third means of escape is through Strength and Energy of character. It consists in destroying life when we have perceived that it is an evil and an absurdity. . . . The fourth means of escape is through Weakness. It consists in continuing to drag on, though the evil and absurdity of life are well known, though aware that nothing can come of it. . . . Thus do those of my own class, in four different ways, save themselves from a terrible contradiction.

Then I thought to myself; 'But what if there be something more for me to know? Mankind as a whole have always lived, and are living, as if they understood the meaning of life, for, not doing so, they could not live at all; and yet I say that all this life has no meaning in it and that I cannot live.' Our wisdom, indeed, the wisdom of the wise, however firmly it be grounded on truth, has not imparted to us a knowledge of the meaning of life; yet all the unwise millions that share in the life of humanity do not doubt that life has a meaning. . . . Whether thanks to my strange kind of instinctive affection for the labouring classes, which impelled me to understand them and to see that they are not so stupid as we think, or thanks to the sincerity of my conviction that I could know nothing beyond the advisability of hanging myself, I felt that, if I wished to live and understand the meaning of life, I must seek it not amongst those who have lost their grasp on it, and wish to kill themselves, but among the millions of the living and the dead who have made our life what it is, and on whom now rests the burden of our life and their own. .

So I watched the life common to such enormous numbers of the dead and the living, the life of simple, unlearned, and poor men, and found something quite different. I saw that all these millions, with rare exceptions, did not come under any division of the classification which I had made. . . . It appeared that throughout mankind there was a sense given to the meaning of life which I had neglected and despised. It came to this, that the knowledge based on reason denied a meaning to life, and declined to make it a subject of inquiry, while the meaning given by the millions that form the great whole of humanity was founded on a despised and fallacious knowledge. . . . I was compelled to admit that, besides the reasoning knowledge which I once thought the only true knowledge, there was in every living man another kind of knowledge, an unreasoning one, but which gives a possibility of living—faith.

Faith is the force of life. If a man lives, he believes in something. If he did not believe that there was something to live for, he would not live. If he does not see and understand the unreality of the finite, he believes in the finite; if he sees that unreality, he must believe in the infinite. Without faith there is no life. . . . The conception of an infinite God, of the divinity of the soul, of the way in which the affairs of men are related to God, of the unity and reality of the spirit, man's conception of moral good and evil, these are conceptions worked out through the infinite mental labours of mankind—conceptions without which there would be no life, without which I should not myself exist.

" I began to draw nearer to the believers among the poor, the simple, and the ignorant, the pilgrims, the monks, the sectaries, and the peasants. The doctrines of these men of the people, like those of the pretended believers of my own class, were Christian. Here also much that was superstitious was mingled with the truths of Christianity, but with this difference: that the superstition of the believers of my own class was not needed by them, and never influenced their lives beyond serving as a kind of Epicurean distraction, while the superstition of the believing labouring class was so interwoven with their lives that it was impossible to conceive them without it—it was a necessary condition of their living at all. The whole life of the believers of my own class was in flat contradiction with their faith, and the whole life of the believers of the people was a confirmation of the meaning of life which their faith gave them. ... In contradiction to the theory that the less learned we are the less we understand the meaning of life, and see in our sufferings and death but an evil joke, these men of the people live, suffer, and drawn ear to death in quiet confidence and oftenest with joy. In contradiction to the fact that an easy death, without terror or despair, is a rare exception in my own class,—a death which is uneasy, rebellious, and sorrowful is among the people the rarest exception of all. These men, deprived of all that for us and for Solomon makes the only good in life, experience the highest happiness both in amount and kind.

I began to grow attached to these men. The more I learned of their lives, the lives of the living and of the dead of whom I read and heard, the more I liked them, and the easier I felt it so to live. I lived in this way during two years, and then there came a change which had long been preparing in me, and the symptoms of which I had always dimly felt. The life of my own circle of rich and learned men not only became repulsive, but lost all meaning whatever. All our actions, our reasoning, our science and art, all appeared to me in a new light. I understood that it was all child's play, that it was useless to seek a meaning in it. The life of the working classes, of the whole of mankind, of those that create life, appeared to me in its true significance. I understood that this was life itself, and that the meaning given to this life was a true one, and I accepted it.

I understood that I had erred, and how I had erred. I had erred not so much through having thought incorrectly as through having lived ill. . . . What had I done during my thirty years of conscious life? I had not only not helped the life of others, I had done nothing for my own, I had lived the life of a parasite, and contented myself with my ignorance of the reason why I lived at all. If the meaning of the life of man lies in his having to work out his life himself, how could I, who during thirty years had done my best to ruin my own life and that of others, expect to receive any other answer to my questioning of life but this, that my life was an evil and had no meaning in it? It *was* an evil; it *was* without meaning.

After this I began to retrace the process which had

gone on within myself, the hundred-times-repeated discouragement and revival. . . . I returned, as it were, to the past, to childhood and my youth. I returned to faith in that Will which brought me into being, and which required something of me; I returned to the belief that the one single aim of life should be to become better, that is, to live in accordance with that Will; I returned to the idea that the expression of that Will was to be found in what, in the dim obscurity of the past, the great human unity had fashioned for its own guidance; in other words, I returned to a belief in God, in moral perfectibility, and in the tradition which gives a meaning to life. The difference was that formerly I had unconsciously accepted this, whereas now I knew that without it I could not live.

Though many things belonging to the faith of the people appeared strange to me, I accepted everything. I attended the Church services, prayed morning and evening, fasted, prepared for the communion; and while doing all this, for the first time felt that my reason found nothing to object to.

It was so necessary for me at that time to believe in order to live, that I unconsciously concealed from myself the contradictions and the obscurities in the commonly-received doctrines. . . . I shall never forget the painful feeling I experienced when I took the communion for the first time after many years. The service, the confession, the prayers, all this was understood by me, and produced the glad conviction that the meaning of life lay open to me. The communion I explained to myself as an action done in remembrance of Christ, and as signifying a cleansing from sin and a complete acceptance of Christ's teaching. . . . But when I drew near to the altar, and the priest called upon me to repeat that I believed that what I was about to swallow was the real body and blood, I felt a sharp pain at the heart; it was no unconsidered word, it was the hard demand of one who could never have known what faith was. I humbled myself again, I swallowed the blood and the body without any mocking thoughts, in the wish to believe; but the shock had been given, and knowing what awaited me another time, I could never go again.

Notwithstanding all my doubts and sufferings, I still remained in the Orthodox Church; but practical questions arose which required immediate decision, and the decisions of the Church, contrary to the elementary principles of the faith by which I lived, compelled me finally to abandon all communion with it. The questions were, in the first place, the relation of the Orthodox Church to other Churches, to Catholicism and the so-called sectarians.

I read everything I could get on the subject, and consulted with as many as I could, but the only explanation I obtained was that of the hussar who accounts his regiment the first in the world, while his friend the lancer says the same of his own. . . . The second point, which concerned the relations of the Church to the problems of life, was her connection with war and executions. . . . When I looked around me at all that was done in the name of religion, I was horrified, and almost entirely withdrew from the Orthodox Church. I looked round on all that was done by men who professed to be Christians, and I was horrified. . . . I

CONVERSION 83

from this time became firmly convinced that all was not truth in the faith which I had joined. Formerly I should have said that all in this faith was false, but now it was impossible to say so.

Whence, then, came this truth and this falsehood? Both the falsehood and the truth came to the people from what is called the Church; both are included in the so-called sacred traditions and writings. I was thus, whether I would or not, brought to the study and analysis of these writings and traditions, a study which, up to that time, I had feared; and I turned to the study of theology, which I had once thrown aside with contempt as useless. . . . I would not attempt to explain everything. I knew that the explanation of the whole, like the beginning of all things, was hidden in infinity. I wished to be brought to the inevitable limit where the incomprehensible begins; I wished that what remained uncomprehended should be so not because the mental impulse to inquiry was not just and natural—all such impulses are, and without them I could understand nothing—but because I had learned the limits of my own mind. I wished to understand so that every unexplained proposition should appear to my reason necessarily unexplainable, and not an obligatory part of belief. I never doubted that the doctrines contained both truth and falsehood, and I was bound to separate the one from the other. I began to do this. What I found of false and true and to what results I came, forms the second part of this work [*i.e.*, 'What I Believe' or 'My Religion'].

All the contradictions, absurdities and cruelties (of conventional religion) I exposed in detail in my work

The Criticism of Dogmatic Theology, where all the Church dogmas and theses as taught in our theology are examined in sequence.—*My Confession.*

At this point salvation came—salvation, which was this. From childhood I had retained a vague idea that in the Gospel lay an answer to the problem before me. In this Gospel teaching, despite all misrepresentations of it in the teaching of the Christian Churches, I felt the presence of truth; and as a last effort, putting aside all interpretations, I began to read and study the Gospel and penetrate its meaning. The further I penetrated the more clearly a new understanding of the Gospel was revealed to me, quite different from that taught by the Christian Churches, and solving the problem of my life.

At length this solution became perfectly clear, and not only clear, but incontestable as well; because, firstly, it harmonised entirely with the demands of my reason and heart, and secondly, when I came to understand it, I saw that this was not my exclusive interpretation of the Gospel (as it might appear), nor even the exclusive revelation of Christ, but the very solution of the problem of life given more or less explicitly by the best among men both before and after the Gospel was given—a succession from Moses, Isaiah, Confucius, the early Greeks, Buddha, Socrates, down to Pascal, Spinoza, Fichte, Feuerbach, and all those, often unnoticed and unknown, who, taking no teachings on trust, thought and spoke sincerely upon the meaning of life. I became confirmed in this truth, and at peace; and I have since with gladness passed through twenty years of life, and am with gladness drawing near to death.—*The Christian Teaching.*

CONVERSION

Having pased the greater part of my life in the country, I came, in the year 1881, to reside in Moscow, where I was immediately struck with the extreme state of pauperism in that city. Though well acquainted with the privations of the poor in rural districts, I had not the faintest conception of their actual condition in towns. In Moscow it is impossible to pass a street without meeting beggars of a kind quite unlike those in the country, who go about there, as the saying is, 'with a bag and the name of Christ.' The Moscow beggars neither carry a bag nor ask for alms. In most cases, when they meet you, they only try to catch your eye, and act according to the expression of your face. . . . I have been deceived by those who stated that they only wanted work, or to buy a ticket in order to return home. Many of them I came to know well, and they knew me, though occasionally, having forgotten me, they would repeat the same false tale. Still these poor rogues were very much to be pitied: they were all ragged, hungry paupers, they are of the sort who die of cold in the streets or hang themselves to escape living.

One cold windy afternoon in December I went to the Khitrof Market, the centre of the town pauperism. . . . I stood behind a file of men at the entrance to the 'Liapin free night-lodging-house.' Those nearest stared at me, the expression in the eyes of all seeming to say, ' Why have you, a man from another world, stopped here with us? Who are you? Are you a self-satisfied man of wealth, desiring to be gladdened by the sight of our need to divert yourself in your idleness, and to mock at us, or are you that which does not and cannot exist—a man who pities us? . . .' It seemed as if each face were more pitiful, harassed, and degraded than the other. I distributed all the money I had—only about twenty roubles—and entered the lodging-house with the crowd. . . . I went first into the women's dormitory— a large room with beds like the berths in a third-class railway carriage ranged in two tiers one above the other. Strange-looking women in ragged dresses, without jackets, old and young, kept coming in and occupying places. Some laughed and swore. I went upstairs. There, in a similar way, the men had taken their places. Among them I recognised one of those to whom I had given money. On seeing him I suddenly felt horribly ashamed and made haste to leave. With a sense of having committed some crime I returned home. There I entered along the carpeted steps into the rug-covered hall, and having taken off my fur coat, sat down to a meal of five courses served by two footmen in livery with white ties and white gloves. . . .' And I realised, not only with my brain but in every pulse of my soul, that whilst there were thousands of such sufferers in Moscow, I, with tens of thousands of others, filled myself daily to repletion with luxurious dainties of every description, took the tenderest care of my horses, and clothed my very floors with velvet carpets.

The town life, which had previously seemed alien and strange to me, became now so hateful that all the indulgences of a luxurious existence, in which I had formerly delighted, now served to torment me. . . . But the first keen sense of self-reproach and shame was blunted, and was replaced by a sense of satisfaction at my own virtue and a desire to make it known to others. . . . And I began to arrange a plan of philanthropic activity in which I might exhibit all my virtues. The census seemed to offer a good opportunity. . . . I

CONVERSION 87

began to collect money and enlist men who wished to help in the work, and who would, in company with the census officers, visit all the nests of pauperism, entering into relations with the poor, finding out the details of their needs, helping them with money and work, sending them out of Moscow, placing their children in schools and their old men and women in homes and houses of refuge. . . . Having invented this plan, I wrote an article about it, and read a proof-copy at a census meeting in the Town Hall, hesitatingly, and blushing till my cheeks burned again, so uncomfortable did I feel. I saw that all my hearers felt equally uncomfortable. Afterwards I spoke to each district manager separately; their look seemed to say, 'Why, out of personal regard for you we have listened to your silly proposition; but here you come out with it again!'

The unfortunate people in the lodging-houses ranged themselves in my mind under three heads: first, those who had lost former advantageous positions and were waiting to recover them (such men belonged to the lowest as well as the highest classes of society); secondly, women of the town, who are very numerous in these houses, and thirdly, children. The majority of these, I found, were of the first class. Unfortunately I did not at first see that such people needed to be relieved, not by my charity, but of their own views of the world. . . . The second class of unfortunates were very numerous and of every kind, from young girls still bearing some likeness to women, to old and fearful-looking creatures without a vestige of humanity. . . . In the third compartment, I asked the woman in a pink dressing-gown about the man who was asleep. She replied that he was a visitor. I asked her who she was. She replied that she was a peasant girl from the county of Moscow. 'What is your occupation?' She laughed and made no answer. 'What do you do for a living?' I repeated, thinking she had not understood the question. 'I sit in the inn,' she said. I did not understand, and asked again. She gave no answer, but continued to giggle. In the fourth room I heard the voices of women also giggling. The landlord turned to the woman and, as one would speak to a dog, said, 'Don't be a fool! speak plainly and say you are a prostitute. She does not even yet know her proper name,' he said, turning to me. This manner of speaking shocked me. . . . I do not remember exactly what I said. I remember only that I was disgusted by the disdainful tones of this young landlord in a lodging filled with females whom he termed prostitutes; and I pitied the woman, and expressed both feelings. No sooner had I said this than I heard from the small compartment where the giggling had been the noise of creaking bed-boards, and over the partition, which did not reach to the ceiling, appeared the disbevelled curly head of a female with small swollen eyes and a shining red face; and a second, and then a third head followed. They were evidently standing on their beds, and all three were stretching their necks and holding their breath and looking silently at me with strained attention. . . . It was like the field of battle covered with dead bones seen by the prophet Ezekiel, on which, trembling from contact with the spirit, the dead bones began to move. They continued to look at me as if wondering what would come next, as if waiting for me to say those words and do those acts by which these dry bones would begin to come together, be covered with flesh and receive life. But I felt, alas! that I had no such words or deeds to give.

I discovered in my visits what I had in no way expected to see. On the one hand I saw in these dens (as I had at first called them) men whom it was impossible for me to help because they were working men, accustomed to labour and privation, and therefore having a much firmer hold on life than I had. On the other hand I saw miserable men whom I could not aid because they were just such as I was myself. The majority of the poor whom I saw were wretched merely because they had lost the capacity, desire, and habit of earning their bread; in other words, their misery consisted in the fact that they were just like myself. My principal conviction now was that with money I could never reform that life of misery which these people led. . . . I became convinced on the one hand that we rich people do not wish and are also unable to distribute to the poor a portion of our superfluities (we have so many wants ourselves) and that money should not be given to anyone if we really wished to do good. So I dropped the affair entirely and quitted Moscow in despair for my own village.—*What must We do Then?*

IV.—Contra Mundum

Having come to the practical conclusion that a man's first duty is to do his own physical labour, I was struck by the ease and simplicity of the solution of all those problems which had formerly seemed to me so difficult and complicated. . . . In answer to the question, 'Is it necessary to organise this physical labour, to establish a society in a village upon this basis?' it appeared that it was not at all necessary to do all this; that if the labour does not aim at rendering idleness possible, and at utilising other men's labour, as is the case with men who save up money, but merely the satisfying of necessities, then such labour will naturally induce people to leave towns for the country, where this labour is most agreeable and productive. There was also no need to establish a society, because a working man will naturally associate with other working people. . . . In answer to the question, 'Would not this labour take up all my time, and would it not deprive me of the possibility of that mental activity which I am so fond of, and to which I have become accustomed, and which in moments of self-conceit I considered to be useful to others?' the answer will be quite an unexpected one. In proportion to bodily exercise the energy of my mental activity increased, having freed itself from all that was superfluous. . . . · The more intense my physical labour was the more it approached that which is considered the hardest—agricultural labour—the more I acquired enjoyments and knowledge, the closer and more affectionate was my intercourse with mankind and the more happiness did I feel in life. . . . It appeared that as soon as I had made physical labour the ordinary condition of my life, then at once the greater part of my false and expensive habits and wants ceased of themselves, without any endeavour on my part.· To say nothing of the habit of turning day into night, and *vice versâ*, of my bedding, clothes, my conventional cleanliness, which all became impossible and embarrassing when I began to labour physically, both the quantity and the quality of my food were totally changed. Instead of the sweet, rich, delicate, complicated, and highly-spiced food, which I was formerly fond of, I now required and obtained plain food as the most agreeable,—sour cabbage soup, porridge, black bread, tea with a bit of sugar. . . . The harder I worked the stronger, sounder, more cheerful and kind I felt myself. When I had plainly understood all this, it became to me ridiculous that I, through a long series of doubt, research, and much thinking, had arrived at this extraordinary truth, that if man has eyes, they are to be seen through; ears, to hear by; feet, to walk with, and hands and back to work with—and that if man will not use these, his members, for what they are meant, then it will be worse for him.—*What must We do Then?*

While offering [in 'What is Art?'] as examples of art those that seem to me the best, I attach no special importance to my selection; for, besides being insufficiently informed in all branches of art, I belong to the class of people whose taste has, by false training, been perverted. And therefore my old, inured habits may cause me to err, and I may mistake for absolute merit the impression a work produced on me in my youth. My only purpose in mentioning examples of works of this or that class is to make my meaning clearer, and to show how, with my present views, I understand excellence in art in relation to its subject-matter. I must, moreover, mention that I consign my own artistic productions to the category of bad art, excepting the story *God sees the Truth*, which seeks a place in the first class (Christian Art), and *The Prisoner of the Caucasus*, which belongs to the second (Universal Art).—*What is Art?*

From the time, twenty years ago, when I first clearly perceived how happily mankind should and might live, and how senselessly they torment themselves and ruin generation after generation, I have kept removing further and further back the fundamental cause of this folly and ruin. At first, fallacious economic organisations appeared to be the cause ; then State coercion, which upholds these organisations ; whereas I have now come to the conviction that the fundamental cause of it all is the erroneous religious teaching transmitted by education. — *The Religious Education of the Young.*

I was at first disinclined to reply to the decision of the Holy Synod concerning myself [The decree of February 25, 1901 O.S.], but that decision has called forth a great many letters. Some of these abuse me for rejecting what I do not reject, others exhort me to believe in what I have never ceased to believe, while others again express an agreement in thought which in fact hardly exists, or a sympathy which I cannot fairly claim. . . . The decision of the Synod has many drawbacks. It is either illegal or intentionally ambiguous, because if it was meant to be an excommunication from the Church it does not correspond with those Church rules according to which an excommunication may be pronounced. And it has been understood as an excommunication. It is arbitrary because it charges me alone with not believing all those points enumerated, while in fact nearly all educated people share this non-belief, and I have constantly expressed, and still express it in conversation, reading, pamphlets and books. . . . It contains manifest untruth, as it asserts that attempts to bring me to reason were made by the Church which, however, were not crowned with success. Nothing of the kind ever happened. It presents what in juridical language is called slander, because it contains unjust statements, knowingly made and circulated to injure me. And lastly, it is an incitement to bad feeling and bad action, since it has, as might have been expected, called forth among unenlightened and unreasoning people anger and hatred toward me, going so far as threats of murder.

That I have abjured the Church which terms itself Orthodox is quite true, but this I did not because I rebelled against, but, on the contrary, because I wished to serve God with all the powers of my soul. Before abjuring the Church and unity with the people, which unity was inexpressibly dear to me, I devoted several years to the investigation of the teachings of the Church, both theoretical and practical . . . and I became convinced that the teaching theoretically is an insidious and injurious lie, while practically it is a collection of the grossest superstitions and sorcery, which entirely obscure all the teachings of Christianity. True I have abjured the Church. I have ceased to observe its rites, and given instructions in my will that my near ones should not allow the servants of the Church to come near me when dying and that my corpse should be as quickly as possible taken away without any conjurations or prayers over it, just as any objectionable and unnecessary thing is taken away so as not to be in the way of the living.

Here is what I do believe: I believe in God, whom I understand as Spirit, as Love, and as the source of everything. I believe that He is in me and I in Him. I believe that the will of God has been expressed in the clearest and most intelligible way in the teaching of the man Christ, to conceive of whom as God and to pray to him I consider the greatest sacrilege. I believe that the real happiness of man consists in men loving one another. . . . I believe that the meaning of every man's life thus consists in increasing love within himself, and that increase of love leads the individual man to greater and greater happiness. . . . At the same time it helps on more than anything else the establishment in the world of the kingdom of God, that is, such a structure of life that discord, deceit, and violence, which now reign, will be replaced by free consent, truth, and fraternal love among men. I believe that there is only one means for the progress of love—prayer, not that public prayer in temples which was directly forbidden by Christ (Matt. vi. 5-13), but the prayer the example of which was given us by Christ, prayer in solitude, consisting in the renovation and strengthening in our consciousness of the meaning of our lives, as also of our dependence on God's will alone.—*Letter in Reply to the Holy Synod.*

This solution of the meaning of my life, which gives me full rest and joy of life, I desire to communicate to men. My age and state of health are such that I am with one foot in the grave, and worldly considerations have no meaning for me. Even had they, I know that this exposition of my religion ['The Christian Teaching'] will not contribute either to my worldly profit or my reputation, but, on the contrary, may only exasperate and grieve both those unbelievers in religion who request literary work from me and not theological treatises, and those believers in religion who are indignant at all my religious writings and abuse me for them. So that I am urged to do what I do, not by wish for gain or fame nor by any worldly considerations, but only by fear to fail in what is required from me by Him who has sent me into this world and to Whom I am hourly expecting to return.

I therefore beg all those who shall read this to follow and understand my writing, putting aside, as I have done, all worldly considerations, and holding before them only that eternal Principle of truth and right by Whose will we have come into the world, whence, as beings in the body, we shall very soon disappear: without hurry or irritation let them understand and judge what I say. If they disagree let them correct me; not with contempt and hatred, but with pity and love. If they agree let them remember that if I speak truth that truth is not mine but God's, and only casually part of it passes through me, just as it passes through every one of us when we behold truth and transmit it to others.—*The Christian Teaching.*

CHAPTER II

SOCIETY

I.—The State in an Age of Violence

However conscious a man may be of the new design and purpose revealed to him by his reason, he goes on in the old fashion until his life has become intolerably inconsistent and therefore distressing.

Humanity has outgrown its social, its civic age, and has entered upon a new epoch. . . . One needs but to compare the practice of life with its theory to be horrified at the extraordinary contradictions between the conditions of life and our inner consciousness. Man's whole life is a continual contradiction of what he knows to be his duty. This contradiction prevails in every department of life, in the economical, the political, and the international.

The man of education suffers even more than a workman from these inconsistencies. If he has any faith whatever he believes, perhaps in fraternity—at least in the sentiment humanity; and if not in the sentiment humanity, then in justice, and if not in justice, then surely in science; and he cannot help knowing all the while that the conditions of his life are opposed to every principle of Christianity, humanity, justice and science. He affirms his faith in the principles of fraternity, humanity, justice, and political science, and yet the oppression of the working class is an indispensable factor in his daily life, and he constantly employs it to attain his own ends, in spite of his principles; and he not only lives in this manner, but he devotes all his energies to maintain a system which is directly opposed to all his beliefs.

We are brothers, but every morning my brother or my sister performs for me the most menial offices. We are brothers, but I must have my morning cigar, my sugar, my mirror, or what not,—objects whose manufacture has often cost my brothers and sisters their health, yet I do not for that reason forbear to use these things, on the contrary, I even demand them. We are brothers, and yet I support myself by working in some bank, commercial house, or shop, and am always trying to raise the price of the necessities of life for my brothers and sisters. We are brothers; 'I receive a salary for judging, convicting, and punishing the thief or the prostitute, whose existence is the natural outcome of my own system of life;' and I fully realise that I should neither condemn nor punish. We are all brothers, yet I make my living by collecting taxes from the poor, that the rich may live in luxury and idleness. We are brothers, and yet I receive a salary for preaching a pseudo-Christian doctrine, in which I do not myself believe, thus hindering men from discovering the true one. I receive a salary as priest or bishop for deceiving people in a matter which is of vital importance to them. We are brothers, but 'I make my brother pay for all my services, whether I write books for him, educate him, or prescribe for him as a physician. We are all brothers, but I receive a salary for fitting myself to be a murderer, for learning the act of war, or for manufacturing arms and ammunition and building fortresses. The whole existence of our upper classes is utterly contradictory, and the more sensitive a man's nature the more painful is the incongruity. A man with a sensitive conscience can enjoy no peace of mind in such a life. . . . Hence our wealthy classes, whether their consciences be tender or hardened, cannot enjoy the advantages they have wrung from the poor as did the ancients, who were convinced of the justice of their position. All the pleasures of life are poisoned either by remorse or fear. Such is the economic inconsistency.

Still more striking is the inconsistency of the civil power. A man is trained first of all in habits of obedience to State laws. At the present time every act of our lives is under the supervision of the State. What is this law that determines the life of mankind? In most cases men recognise its injustice; they despise it, and yet they obey it. It was fitting that the ancients should obey their law. It was chiefly religious, and they sincerely believed it to be the only true law to which all men owed obedience. Is that the case with us? Men have long since realised that there is no sense in obeying a law whose honesty is more than doubtful, and therefore they must suffer when, though privately denying its prerogative, they still conform to it. We recognise the disadvantages of custom-houses and import duties, but we are yet obliged to pay them; we see the folly of supporting the Court and its numerous officials, we admit the harmful influence of Church preaching, and still we are compelled to support both; we also admit the cruel and iniquitous punishments inflicted by the courts, and yet we play our part in them; we acknowledge that the distribution of land is wrong and immoral, but we have to submit to it; and despite the fact that we deny the necessity for armies or warfare, we are made to bear the heavy burden of supporting armies and waging war.

The advocates of the social life-conception usually attempt to combine the idea of authority, otherwise violence, with that of moral influence; but such a union is utterly impossible. The result of moral influence upon man is to change his desires, so that he willingly complies with what is required of him, whereas authority, as the word is commonly understood, is a means of coercion, by which a man is forced to act in opposition to his wishes. In order to force a man to do something for which he has an aversion, the threat of physical violence, or violence itself, must be employed; he may be deprived of his liberty, flogged, mutilated, or he may be threatened with these punishments. And this is what constitutes power both in the past and in the present. . . . All the requisitions of the State, such as the payment of taxes and the fulfilment of public duties, the submission to penalties in the form of exile, fines, etc., to which men seem to yield voluntarily, are always enforced by the physical threat or the reality of physical punishment. Physical violence is the basis of authority. It is the military organisation that makes it possible to inflict physical violence, that organisation wherein the entire armed force acts as one man, obeying a single will. . . . Neither congresses, parliaments, senates, nor any other means of restraint have yet proved effectual. No expedient has been found to commit authority to infallible men or to prevent its abuses. On the contrary, we know that men who have the authority always are more liable to become immoral, to put their own interests first, than those who have not. Therefore it is that the evil principle of violence relegated to authority is ever increasing, and the evil becomes in time worse than that which it is supposed to control; whereas in the individual members of society the inclination to violence is always diminishing, and the violence of authority becomes less and less necessary.

It is not enough that all men bound by the organisation of the State transfer their responsibility from one to the other—the peasant, for instance, who becomes a soldier, to the merchant who has become an officer; the officer to the noble who occupies the position of Governor; the Governor to the Minister of State; the Minister to the Sovereign; and the Sovereign, who in his turn shifts the responsibility upon all, officials, nobles, merchants, peasants—they so constantly, persistently and strenuously assure themselves and others that all men are not equal that they begin to believe it sincerely themselves.

It is to this inequality—the exaltation of some by the abasement of others—that we may chiefly attribute men's inability to discern the folly of the existing system, with the cruelty and deceptions committed by some and suffered by others. There are certain men who have been made to believe that they are possessed of a peculiar importance and greatness, who have become so intoxicated by their imaginary superiority that they cease to realise their responsibility for the actions they commit; others who, on the contrary, have been told that they are insignificant beings, and that it is their duty to submit to those above them, and, as the natural result of this continual state of degradation, fall into a strange condition of stupefied servility, and in this state they too lose all sense of responsibility for their actions. And as to the intermediate class, they are apt to be both servile and arrogant, and they also lose the sense of responsibility. . . . It is this delusion in regard to human inequality and the consequent intoxication of power and stupefaction of servility that make it possible for those associated in a State organisation to commit crimes and suffer no remorse.—*The Kingdom of God is Within You.*

Before one gives money for the establishment of internal order and social institutions, one must be sure that the people who are to establish this order will really do it; and also that the order itself will be good, and the proposed social institutions indeed necessary for the community. If, on the contrary (which has been the case always and everywhere), the payers of taxes do not believe either in the capacity or even in the honesty of those who maintain the said system, and, besides, consider the system itself evil and the proposed social institutions utterly unsuited to the needs of the taxpayers, then it is evident that there can exist no right to levy taxes, but only violence.

We see numberless administrators—the sovereign, his brothers and uncles, ministers, judges, and clergy—receiving enormous sums gathered from the people, and not even fulfilling those light duties undertaken in exchange for their remuneration. It appears, then, they steal these salaries, gathered from the people, and therefore the people's property—and yet it does not enter the head of anyone to condemn them.

Yet taxation, the usurpation of land, and the power of capitalists, do not constitute the fundamental cause of the miserable condition of the working classes, but only the consequences. 'The essential reason why millions of working men live and labour under the orders of the minority is not that the minority has usurped the land and the instruments of labour, and gathers taxes, but that it has the power to do so, because there is violence, and because there is an army, which is in the hands of the minority, and is ready to kill those who refuse to obey the will of that minority. . . . The workmen wish to free themselves, and yet they themselves force each other to submit, and to remain in slavery! Why do they do this? They do it because all the workmen, enlisted or hired as soldiers, are subjected to a skilful process of stupefaction and degradation, after which they cannot help submitting blindly to their superiors, whatever they may be ordered to do. . . . Therefore the existence of the army is also not the fundamental cause, but only the consequence. The first cause is the doctrine which teaches men that military service, the aim of which is only murder, is not a sinless, but even a commendable, admirable, and heroic occupation.

When the Pagan monarchs Constantine, Charlemagne, and Valdimir, adopted Christianity clothed in the forms of Paganism, and christened their peoples in it, they did not dream that the teaching they accepted destroyed the power of kings, the army, and the State itself. But the more Christian the peoples lived, the more clearly manifest became the essence of Christianity, and the more evident grew the danger to Paganism it presented. And the greater that danger grew, the more laboriously did the ruling classes try to stifle, and, if possible, to quench, the light they unconsciously brought into the world with Christianity. For this purpose they used all possible means: prohibition to read or translate the Gospels; slaughter of all who point out the true meaning of Christian teaching; hypnotism of the masses by the pomp and splendour of rituals; and especially hair-splitting and equivocal distortions of Christian precepts. In proportion as these methods were employed, Christianity became more and more modified, till at last it became a teaching which not only did not contain any principles destructive to the Pagan system of life, but, on the contrary, justified that system from a pseudo-Christian standpoint. There appeared Christian monarchs, and Christian armies, and Christian wealth, and Christian law-courts, and Christian executions.—*The Root of the Evil.*

Other contradictions are but trifling in comparison with the one which confronts us in the problem of our international relations, and which cries aloud for solution, since both human reason and human life are at stake, and this is the antagonism between the Christian faith and war. We, Christian nations, whose spiritual life is one and the same, who welcome the birth of every wholesome and profitable thought with joy and pride, from whatsoever quarter of the globe it may spring, regardless of race or creed; we, who love not only the philanthropists, the poets, the philosophers and the scientists of other lands; we, who take as much pride in the heroism of a Father Damien as if it was our own; we, who love the French, the Germans, the Americans and the English, not only esteeming their qualities, but ready to meet them with cordial friendship; we, who not only would be shocked to consider war with them in the light of an exploit—when we picture to ourselves the possibility that at some future day a difference may arise between us that can only be reconciled by murder, and that any one of us may be called upon to play his part in an inevitable tragedy, we shudder at the thought. It was well enough for a Hebrew, a Greek, or a Roman to maintain the independence of his country by murder, and even to subdue other nations by the same means, because he firmly believed himself a member of the one favoured people beloved by God, and that all the others were Philistines and barbarians. Also, in the times of the Middle Ages men well might have held these opinions, and even they who lived towards the end of the 18th century and at the beginning of the last. But, whatever provocation may be offered us, we cannot possibly believe as they did; and this difficulty is so painful for us in these times that it has become impossible to live without trying to solve it.

It is the popular belief that governments increase armies as a means of defence against other nations, forgetting that troops are principally needed by governments to protect them against their own enslaved subjects. This has always been necessary, and has grown more so with the spread of education, the increase of intercourse among different nationalities; and at the present time, in view of the communist, socialist, anarchist, and labour movements, it is a more urgent necessity than ever. Governments realise this fact and increase their principal means of defence—the disciplined army. . . . Armies have reached the millions which they now number not only from the fear of foreign invasion; the increase was first caused by the necessity for putting down all attempts at rebellion on the part of the subjects of the State. The one depends upon the other. The despotism of governments increases exactly in proportion to the increase of their strength and their internal successes, and their foreign aggression with the increase of internal despotism. European governments try to outdo one another, ever increasing their armaments, and compelled at last to adopt the expedient of a general conscription as a means of enrolling the greatest number of troops at the smallest possible expense. . . . Thus all the citizens took up arms to assist in upholding the wrongs that were committed against them; in fact, they became their own oppressors. Every man who yields to military conscription becomes an involuntary participator in all the oppressive acts of the government towards its subjects.

The existing governments and the ruling classes no longer care to present even the semblance of justice, but rely, thanks to scientific progress, on an organisation so ingenious that it is able to enclose all men within a circle of violence through which it is impossible to break. This circle is made up of four expedients, each connected with and supporting the other like the rings of a chain. The first and the oldest expedient is intimidation. It consists in representing the actual organisation of the State, whether it be that of a liberal republic or of an arbitrary despotism, as something sacred and immutable, which therefore punishes by the most cruel penalties any attempt at revolution. . . . The second expedient is bribery. This consists in taking the property of the labouring classes by means of taxation and distributing it among the officials, who, in consideration of this, are bound to maintain and increase the bondage of the people. . . . The third expedient I can call by no other name than hypnotism. It consists in retarding the spiritual development of men, and, by means of various suggestions, influencing them to cling to the theory of life which mankind has already left behind, and upon which rests the foundation of governmental authority. . . . The fourth expedient consists in this: certain individuals are selected from among the mass of enslaved and stupefied beings; and these, after having been subjected to a still more vigorous process of brutalisation, are made the passive instruments of the cruelties and brutalities indispensable to the government. This state of brutality and imbecility is produced by taking men in their youth, before they have yet had time to gain any clear conception of morality; and then, having removed them from all the natural conditions of human life, from home, family, birthplace, and the possibility of intelligent labour, by shutting them up together in barracks, where, dressed in a peculiar uniform, to the accompaniment of shouts, drums, music, and the display of glittering gewgaws, they are daily forced to perform certain prescribed evolutions. By these methods they are reduced to that hypnotic condition when they cease to be men and become imbecile and docile machines in the hands of the hypnotiser. These physically strong young men thus hypnotised (and at the present time, with the general conscription system, all young men answer to this description), supplied with murderous weapons, ever obedient to the authority of the government, and ready at its command to commit any violence whatsoever, constitute the fourth and the principal means for subjugating men. So the circle of violence is completed.

In 1891, Kaiser Wilhelm, the *enfant terrible* of State authority, who expresses what other men only venture to think, in a talk with certain soldiers, uttered publicly the following words, which were repeated the next day in thousands of papers:—'You have taken the oath of allegiance to *me;* this means, children of my Guards, that you are now *my* soldiers, that you have given yourselves up to me, body and soul. But one enemy exists for you—*my* enemy. With the present socialistic intrigues *it may happen that I shall command you to shoot your own relatives, your brothers, even your parents* (from which may God preserve us!), *and then you are in duty bound to obey my orders unhesitatingly.*' This man expresses what is known but carefully concealed by all wise rulers. He says outright that the men who serve in the army serve *him* and *his* advantage, and should be ready for that purpose to kill their brothers and fathers. Roughly but distinctly he lays bare all the horror of the crime for which men who become soldiers prepare themselves—all that abyss of self-abasement into which they fling themselves when they promise obedience. Like a bold hypnotiser, he tests the depth of the slumber; he applies red-hot iron to the sleeper's body; it smokes and shrivels, but the sleeper does not awaken. Poor, sick, miserable man, intoxicated with power, who by these words insults all that is sacred to men of modern civilisation! . . . It would seem as if these insane words, offensive to all that a civilised human being holds sacred, ought to rouse indignation; but nothing of the kind happens. . . . Even by savages certain objects are held sacred, for whose sake they are ready to suffer rather than submit. But what is sacred for the man of the modern world? He is told: be my slave, in a bondage where you may have to murder your own father; and he, oftentimes a man of learning, submissively offers his neck to the halter. He is dressed in a clown's garments, ordered to leap, to make contortions, to salute, to kill, and he submissively obeys; and when at last allowed to return to his former life he continues to hold forth on the dignity of man, freedom, equality and brotherhood.

I was told of an incident which happened to an intrepid *stanovoy*, who, on arriving in a village where the peasants had revolted, and whither troops had been sent, undertook, like the Emperor Nicholas I., to quell the disturbance by his personal influence. He ordered several loads of rods to be brought, and having gathered all the peasants into the barn, he entered himself, shut himself in with them, and so terrified them by his shouts and threats that in compliance with his commands they began to flog each other. And so they went on flogging one another until some fool revolted, and shouting to his comrades, bade them leave off. It was not until then that the flogging ceased and the *stanovoy* escaped from the barn. It is this very advice of the fool that men who believe in the necessity of civil government seem unable to follow. They are unable to stop punishing themselves, and setting an absurd example for others to imitate. Such is the consummation of merely human wisdom.

The progression from love of family to love of race is difficult, and requires special education, which has arrived at its utmost limits when the State has been reached. . . . Love for a nation, Turkey, for instance, or Germany, England, Austria, Russia, is almost impossible, and notwithstanding the training given in that direction, it is only a fictitious semblance; it has no real existence. But the man who loves humanity, what is it that he loves? There is a state, there is a people, there is the abstract conception of man. But humanity as a concrete

THE STATE 109

conception is impossible. . . . If we include all humanity without exception, why should we restrict ourselves to men? Why should we exclude the higher animals, some of whom are superior to the lowest representatives of the human race? We do not know humanity in the concrete, nor can we fix its limits. Humanity is a fiction, and therefore it cannot be loved. . . . Love founded on a personal and social life-conception can go no further than the love of country. The social life-conception has brought men not to the consciousness of love for humanity, but to a condition which evokes no feeling in man, to a contradiction for which it provides no reconciliation.

It is only the Christian doctrine which, by lending to human life a new significance, is able to solve the difficulty. Christianity presents the love of self and the love of the family, as well as patriotism and the love of humanity, but it is not to be restricted to humanity alone; it is to be given to every living creature; it recognises the possibility of an indefinite expansion of the kingdom of love, but its object is not to be found outside itself, in the aggregate of individuals, neither in the family, nor in the race, nor in the state, nor in mankind, nor all the wide world, but in itself, in its personality—a divine personality, whose essence is the very love which needed a wider sphere. Patriotism is a rude, harmful, disgraceful and bad feeling, and above all is immoral. It is a rude feeling, because it is one natural only to people standing on the lowest level of morality, and expecting from other nations those outrages which they themselves are ready to inflict on others; it is a harmful feeling, because it disturbs advantageous and joyous peaceful relations with other peoples, and above all it produces that governmental organisation under which power may fall, and does fall, into the hands of the worst men; it is a disgraceful feeling, because it turns man not merely into a slave, but into a fighting cock, a bull, or a gladiator, who wastes his strength and his life for objects which are not his own but his government's; and it is an immoral feeling, because instead of confessing oneself a son of God, as Christianity teaches us, or even a free man guided by his own reason, each man under the influence of patriotism confesses himself the son of his fatherland and the slave of his government, and commits actions contrary to his reason and his conscience.

This harmful and antiquated feeling not only continues to exist, but burns more and more fiercely. . . . This occurs because the ruling classes can retain their position—exceptionally advantageous in comparison with that of the labouring masses—thanks only to the government organisation, which rests on patriotism. Every official prospers the better in his career the more patriotic he is; so also the army man gets promotion in time of war; and war is produced by patriotism. Patriotism and its result, wars, give an enormous revenue to the newspaper trade, and profits to many other trades. Every writer, teacher and professor is more secure in his place the more he preaches patriotism. Every emperor and king obtains the more fame the more he is addicted to patriotism. The ruling classes have in their hands the army, money, the schools, the churches, and the press. In the schools they kindle patriotism in the children by means of histories describing their own people as the best of all peoples, and always in the right. Among adults they kindle it by spectacles, jubilees, monuments, and by a lying patriotic press. Above all, they inflame patriotism in this way: perpetrating every kind of injustice and harshness against other nations, they provoke in them enmity towards their own people, and then in turn exploit that enmity to embitter their own people against the foreigner.

Since this servile submission of the masses to the calls of patriotism, the audacity, cruelty, and insanity of the governments has known no bounds. A competition in the usurpation of other people's lands in Asia, Africa, and America began—evoked partly by whim, partly by vanity, and partly by covetousness—and has been accompanied by ever greater and greater distrust and enmity between the governments.

It is generally said that the real, good patriotism consists in desiring for one's own people or State such real benefits as do not infringe the well-being of other nations. . . . But the real patriotism, which we all know, by which most people to-day are swayed, and from which humanity suffers so severely, is not the wish for spiritual benefits for one's own people (it is impossible to desire spiritual benefits for one's own people only); but it is a very definite feeling of preference for one's own people or State above all other peoples and States, and therefore it is the wish to get for that people or State the greatest advantages and power that can be got; and these are always obtainable only at the expense of the advantages and power of other peoples or States. It would therefore seem obvious that patriotism as a feeling is a bad and harmful feeling, and as a doctrine is a stupid doctrine. For it is clear that if each people and each State considers itself the best of peoples and States, they all dwell in a gross and harmful delusion.

All the peoples of the so-called Christian world have been reduced by patriotism to such a state of brutality that not only those who are obliged to kill or be killed desire slaughter and rejoice in murder, but all the people of Europe and America, living peaceably in their homes, exposed to no danger, are, at each war—thanks to easy means of communication, and to the press—in the position of the spectators in a Roman circus, and, like them, delight in the slaughter, and raise the bloodthirsty cry, '*Pollice verso.*'—*Patriotism and Government.*

Violence can never suppress that which is countenanced by general custom. If public opinion would but frown upon violence, it would destroy all its power. What would happen if violence were not employed against hostile nations and the criminal element in society we do not know. But that the use of violence subdues neither we do know through long experience. How can we expect to subdue by violence nations whose education, traditions, and even religious training all tend to glorify resistance to the conqueror and love of liberty as the loftiest of virtues? And how is it possible to extirpate crime by violence in the midst of communities where the same act regarded by the government as criminal is transformed into an heroic exploit by public opinion? The power transcending all others which has influenced individuals and nations since time began, that power which is the convergence of the invisible, intangible, spiritual forces of all humanity, is public opinion. Violence serves but to enervate this influence, disintegrating it, and substituting for it one, not only useless, but pernicious to the welfare of humanity.

In order to win over all these outside the Christian

THE STATE

fold, all the Zulus, the Manchurians, the Chinese, whom many consider uncivilised, and the uncivilised among ourselves, there is *only one way*. This is by the diffusion of a Christian mode of thought, which is only to be accomplished by a Christian life, Christian deeds, a Christian example. Instead we steal their territory, sell them wine, tobacco, and opium, and teach them the animal law of strife; having sent them a score of missionaries, who gabble an absurd clerical jargon, we quote the results of our attempt to convert the heathen as an indubitable proof that the truths of Christianity are not adaptable to everyday life.

Those whom we call criminals we imprison, execute, guillotine, hang. We encourage the masses in idolatrous religions calculated to stultify them; the government authorises the sale of brain-destroying poisons—wine, tobacco, opium; prostitution is legalised; we bestow land upon those who need it not; surrounded by misery, we display in our entertainments an unbridled extravagance; we render impossible in such ways any semblance of a Christian life, and do our best to destroy Christian ideas already established; and then, after doing all we can to demoralise men, we take and confine them like wild beasts in places from which they cannot escape, and where they will become more brutal than ever; or we murder the men we have demoralised, and then use them as an example to illustrate and prove our argument that people are only to be controlled by violence.— *The Kingdom of God is Within You*.

'Just such a dangerous creature as yesterday's culprit,' thought Nekhlúdoff. 'They are dangerous; and we who judge them—? I, a rake, an adulterer, a deceiver. We are not dangerous! . . . But even so, what should we do? We seize one such lad, knowing that there are thousands like him whom we have not caught, and send him to prison, where, in company with others weakened and enslaved by the lives they have led, idleness or most unwholesome, useless labour is forced on him. . . . But we do nothing to destroy the conditions in which people like these are produced; on the contrary, we support the establishments where they are formed. These establishments are well known—factories, foundries, workshops, public-houses, gin-shops, brothels. And we do not destroy these places, but, considering them to be necessary, we support and regulate them. . . .' Thus thought Nekhlúdoff with unusual clearness and vividness, sitting in his high-backed chair next to the colonel, listening to the different intonations of the advocates', prosecutor's and president's voices, and looking at their self-confident gestures. 'And how much effort this pretence requires,' continued Nekhlúdoff in his mind, glancing round the enormous room, at the portraits, lamps, armchairs, uniforms, the thick walls and large windows, and picturing to himself the tremendous size of the building and the still more ponderous dimensions of the whole of this organisation, with its armies of officials, scribes, watchmen, messengers, not only in this place, but all over Russia, who receive wages for carrying on this comedy which no one needs. ' Supposing we spent one-hundredth of these efforts on helping these castaways, whom now we regard only as hands and bodies required by us for our own peace and comfort! Had someone chanced to take pity on him and given him some help at the time when poverty made them send him to town, it might have been sufficient,' Nekhlúdoff thought, looking at the boy's piteous face. . . . 'Ill, his constitution undermined by unhealthy labour, drink and debauchery, knocking aimlessly about town, bewildered as in a dream, he gets into some sort of a shed, and takes some old mats which nobody needs; and here we, all of us educated people, rich or comfortably off, meet together, dressed in good clothes and fine uniforms, in a splendid apartment, to mock this unfortunate brother of ours whom we ourselves have ruined. Terrible! It is difficult to say whether the cruelty or the absurdity is greater, but the one and the other seem to be brought to their climax.'

What is this astonishing institution called criminal law, of which the results are that in all those other places of confinement, from the Peter and Paul Fortress in Petersburg to the island of Sakhalín, hundreds and thousands of victims are pining? What does this strange criminal law exist for? How has it originated? From his personal relations with the prisoners, from notes by some of those in confinement, and by questioning the advocate and the prison priest, Nekhlúdoff came to the conclusion that the convicts, the so-called criminals, could be divided into five classes. The first were quite innocent people, condemned by judicial blunders. There were not many of these—according to the priest's words only seven per cent.—but their condition excited particular interest. To the second class belonged persons condemned for actions done under peculiar circumstances, *i.e.*, in a fit of passion, jealousy, or drunkenness; circumstances under which those who judged them would surely have committed the same actions. The third class consisted of people punished for having committed actions which, according to their ideas, were quite natural, and even good, but which those other people, the men who had made the laws, considered to be crimes. Such were the persons who sold spirits without a license, smugglers, those who gathered grass and wood on large estates and in the forests belonging to the Crown, the thieving miners, and those unbelieving people who robbed churches. To the fourth class belonged those who were imprisoned only because they stood morally higher than the average level of society. Such were the sectarians, the Poles, the Circassians rebelling in order to regain their independence, the political prisoners, the Socialists, and the strikers. According to Nekhlúdoff's observations, there were a very large percentage belonging to this class; among them some of the best of men, who, while only defending their rights, were condemned for resisting the authorities. The fifth class consisted of persons who had been far more sinned against by society than they had sinned against it. These were the castaways, stupefied by continual oppression and temptation, those depraved abnormal creatures whom the new school of criminology classify as the criminal type, against which, according to Nekhlúdoff, society had sinned not directly, but through their fathers and forefathers.—*Resurrection.*

When all was ready the Governor bade the first of the twelve men who were pointed out to him by the landowner [as the ringleaders in an attempt to prevent the arrest of their women-folk] to step forward. It so happened that he was the father of a family, a man forty-five years of age, respected in the community, whose rights he had manfully defended. He was led to the bench, stripped and ordered to lie down. He would have begged for mercy, but, realising how little it would avail, he made the sign of the cross and stretched himself out on the bench. Two policemen held him down, and the learned doctor stood by, ready in case of need to give his scientific assistance. The executioners having spat upon their hands, swung the rods, and the flogging began. The bench, it seemed, was too narrow, and another had to be brought, while the half-naked, pale and suffering man, trembling, with contracted brows and downcast eyes, stood by waiting. When the bench was readjusted, he was again stretched out upon it, and the horse-stealers renewed their blows. His back, his legs, and even his sides were covered with bleeding wounds, and every blow was followed by the muffled groan which he could no longer repress. In the crowd that stood by one could hear the sobs of the wife and mother, the children and the kinsfolk of the man, as well as of all who had been called to witness the punishment. The wretched Governor, intoxicated with power, who had no doubt convinced himself of the necessity for this performance, counted the strokes on his fingers, while he smoked cigarette after cigarette, for the lighting of which several obliging persons hastened to offer him a burning match. After fifty blows had been given, the peasant lay motionless, without uttering a sound, and the doctor, who had been educated in a government school, that he might devote his scientific knowledge to the service of his country and his sovereign, approached the tortured man, felt his pulse, listened to the beating of his heart, and reported to the representative of authority that the victim had become unconscious, and declared that, from a scientific point of view, it might prove dangerous to prolong the punishment. But the unfortunate Governor, utterly intoxicated by the sight of blood, ordered the flogging to go on, until seventy strokes had been given, the number which he for some reason deemed necessary. After the seventieth blow the Governor said, 'That will do! Now bring on the next one!' They raised the mutilated and unconscious man with his swollen back and carried him away, and the next was brought forward. The sobs and groans of the crowd increased, but the tortures were continued. So it went on until each of the twelve men had received seventy strokes.—*The Kingdom of God is Within You.*

II.—PROPERTY, LUXURY, AND THE EXPLOITATION OF LABOUR.

Slavery has long been abolished. It was abolished as well in Rome as in America, and among ourselves; but the word only has been abolished, and not the evil. Slavery is the violent freeing of some men from the labour necessary for satisfying their wants, which transfers this labour to others; and wherever there is a man who does not work, not because others willingly and lovingly work for him, but because he has the possibility, while not working himself, to make others work for him, there is slavery. Slavery with its three fundamental modes of operation—personal violence, soldiery, land-taxes maintained by soldiery, and direct and indirect taxes put upon all the inhabitants, and so maintained—is still in operation now as it has been before. We do not see it, because each of these three forms of slavery has received a new justification, which hides its meaning from us.

In our time, property is the root of all evil and of the sufferings of men who possess it, or are without it, and of all the remorse of conscience of those who misuse it, and of the danger from the collision between those who have it, and those who have it not. Property is the root of all evil; and, at the same time, property is that towards which all the activity of our modern society is directed, and that which directs the activity of the world. States and governments intrigue, make wars, for the sake of property, for the possession of the banks of the Rhine, of land in Africa, China, the Balkan Peninsula. Bankers, merchants, manufacturers, landowners, labour, use cunning, torment themselves, torment others, for the sake of property; government functionaries, tradesmen, landlords, struggle, deceive, oppress, suffer for the sake of property; courts of justice and police protect property; penal servitude, prisons, all the terrors of so-called punishments—all is done for the sake of property. Property is the root of all evil; and now all the world is busy with the distribution and protecting of wealth.

On looking at our lives, or at the lives of rich people from without, I saw that all that is considered as the *summum bonum* of these lives consists in being separated as much as possible from the poor, or is in some way or other connected with this desired separation. In fact, all the aim of our lives, beginning with food, dress, dwelling, cleanliness, and ending with our education, consists in placing a gulf between us and them. And in order to establish this distinction and separation we spend nine-tenths of our wealth in erecting impassable barriers. . . . This applies to all the modes of living expressed by the word 'cleanliness.' Cleanliness! Who does not know human beings, especially women, who make a great virtue of cleanliness? Who does not know the various phases of this cleanliness, which have no limit whatever when it is procured by the labour of others? Who among self-made men has not experienced in his own person with what pains he carefully accustomed himself to this cleanliness, which illustrates the saying, 'White hands are fond of another's labour'? To-day cleanliness consists in changing one's shirt daily, and to-morrow it will be changed twice a day. At first, one has to wash one's hands and neck every day, then one will have to wash one's feet every day, and afterwards it will be the whole body, and in peculiar ways. A clean tablecloth serves for two days, then it is changed every day, and afterwards two tablecloths a day are used. To-day the footman is required to have clean hands: to-morrow he must wear gloves, and clean gloves, and he must hand the letters on a clean tray. And there are no limits to this cleanliness, which is of no other use to anyone than to separate us from others, and to make our intercourse with them impossible, while cleanliness is obtained through the labour of others.

Who am I that desire to better men's condition? I desire it; and yet I get up at noon, after having played at cards in a brilliantly lighted saloon during all the previous night, I, an enfeebled and effeminate man, who thus require the help and services of hundreds of people, I come to help them!—these men who rise at five, sleep on boards, feed upon cabbage and bread, understand how to plough, to reap, to put a handle to an axe, to write, to harness horses, to sew; men who, by their strength and perseverance and self-restraint, are a hundred times stronger than I who come to help them. . . . I go to help the poor. But of the two, who is the poorer? No one is poorer than myself. I am a weak, good-for-nothing parasite, who can only exist in very peculiar conditions, who can live only when thousands of people labour to support this life which is not useful to anyone. And I, this very caterpillar which eats up the leaves of a tree, wish to help the growth and the health of the tree, and to cure it!—*What then is to be Done?*

The family snare is used more than any other to justify men's sins. Persons free from the snare of preparation for life, or that of activity, are rarely free— especially if they be women—from the family snare. This consists in men, in the name of exclusive love for the members of their own family, regarding themselves as free from duties to others, and calmly committing sins of avarice, ambition, idleness, and lust without regarding them as sins. The evil of this snare is that, more than any other, it strengthens the sin of property, intensifies strife among men by exalting as a merit and a virtue the animal instinct of love towards one's family, and diverts men from knowledge of the true meaning of life. In order not to fall into this snare, man must understand and remember, firstly, that love is true, bestowing life and welfare, only when it neither seeks, nor expects, nor hopes for recompense, just as no other manifestation of life expects recompense for its existence. Secondly, that love for one's family is an animal instinct, which is good only so long as kept within the limits of an instinct and so long as man does not sacrifice spiritual demands for its sake.—*The Christian Teaching*.

Hundreds of times have I spoken with peasants who live in towns; and from my talks with them, and from my own observations, it became clear to me that the accumulation of country people in our cities is partly necessary, because they could not otherwise earn their livelihood, and partly voluntary, because they are attracted by the temptations of a town life. . . . The cause is a simple one, for property passing from the hands of the agriculturalist into those of non-agriculturalists thus accumulates in towns. The wealth of country producers passes into the hands of tradespeople, landowners, government functionaries, manufacturers. The men who receive this wealth want to enjoy it, and to enjoy it fully they must be in town. In the village, owing to the inhabitants being scattered, it is difficult for the rich to gratify all their desires. Another of the chief pleasures procured by wealth—vanity, the desire to astonish, to make a display before others—cannot be gratified in the country for the same reason. And luxury in the country is even disagreeable to a man who has a conscience, and is an anxiety to a timid person. . . . Therefore rich people gather together in towns, where the enjoyment of all sorts of luxuries is carefully protected by a numerous police. . . . A countryman often cannot help going to town where a ceaseless round of feasting is going on, where what has been procured from the peasants is being spent; he comes into the town in order to feed upon those crumbs which fall from the tables of the rich; and partly by observing the careless, luxurious, and universally approved mode of living of these men, he begins to desire to order his own affairs in such a manner that he, too, may be able to work less and avail himself more of the labour of others. And at last he decides to settle down in the neighbourhood of the wealthy, trying by every means in his power to get back from them what is necessary for him, and submitting to all the conditions which the rich enforce. These country people assist in gratifying all the fancies of the wealthy: they serve them in public baths, in taverns, as coachmen and as prosti-

PROPERTY, LUXURY, SLAVERY 123

tutes. They manufacture carriages, make toys and dresses, and little by little learn from their wealthy neighbours how to live like them, not by real labour, but by all sorts of tricks, squeezing out from others the money they have collected, and so become depraved, and are ruined. It is, then, this same population, depraved by the wealth of towns, which forms that city misery which I wished to relieve, but could not.

I found the clerk reading prayers over the dead laundry-woman. The lodgers, starvelings themselves, had contributed money for the prayers, the coffin, and the shroud. . . . All the dead are beautiful, but this one was particularly so; her face looked weary, but kind, and not sad at all, though rather astonished. And, indeed, if the living do not see, the dead may well be astonished.

On the day I wrote this there was a great ball in Moscow. On the same night I left home after eight o'clock. I live in a locality surrounded by factories; and I left home after the factory whistle had sounded, and when, after a week of incessant work, people were freed for their holiday. Factory-men passed by me, and I by them, all turning their steps to the public-houses and inns. Many were already tipsy: many more were with women. Every morning at five I hear each of the whistles, which means that the labour of women, children, and old people has begun. At eight o'clock another whistle—this means half an hour's rest; at twelve the third whistle—this means an hour for dinner. At eight o'clock the fourth whistle, indicating cessation from work. By a strange coincidence all the three factories in my neighbourhood produce only the articles necessary for balls. One may, on hearing those whistles, attach to them no other meaning than that of the indication of time. But one may associate with them also the meaning they in reality have—that at the first whistle at five o'clock in the morning, men and women, who have slept side by side in a damp cellar, get up in the dark and hurry away into the noisy building, and take their part in a work of which they see neither cessation nor utility for themselves, and work often so in the heat, in suffocating exhalations, with very rare intervals of rest, for one, two, or three, or even twelve or more hours. And so it goes on from one week to another, interrupted only by holidays.

I walked on, observing these workmen in the streets till eleven o'clock. . . . And now from every side carriages appeared, all going in one direction. On the coach-box sat a coachman, sometimes in a sheepskin coat, and a footman—a dandy with a cockade. Well-fed horses, covered with cloth, ran at the rate of fifteen miles an hour; in the carriages sat ladies wrapped in shawls, and taking great care not to spoil their flowers and their toilets. All, beginning with the harness on the horses, carriages, gutta-percha wheels, the cloth of the coachman's coat, down to the stockings, shoes, flowers, velvet, gloves, scents—all these articles have been made by those men, some of whom fell asleep on their own pallets in their mean rooms, some in night-houses with prostitutes, and others in the police-station. The ball-goers drive past these men, in and with things made by them; and it does not even enter into their minds that there could possibly be any connection between the ball they are going to and these tipsy people, to whom their coachmen shout out so angrily. With quite easy minds and assurance that they are doing nothing wrong they enjoy themselves at the ball. We know that each woman at this ball, whose dress costs a hundred and fifty roubles, was not born at the ball, but she has lived also in the country, has seen peasants, knows her own nurse and maid, whose fathers and brothers are poor, for whom earning a hundred and fifty roubles to build a cottage with is the end and aim of a long, laborious life; she knows this; how can she, then, enjoy herself, knowing that on her half-naked body she is wearing the cottage which is the dream of her housemaid's brother?

The work of mowing is one of the most important in the world. If there is more hay there will be also more meat for old people and milk for children. For each mower here is decided the question of bread and milk for himself and for his children during the winter. Each of the working people, male and female, knows it: even the children know that this is an important business, and that one ought to work with all one's strength, carry a jug of kvas for the father to the mowing place, and, shifting it from one hand to another, run barefoot as quickly as possible a distance of perhaps a mile and a half from the village, in order to be in time for dinner, that father may not grumble. Everyone knows that, from the mowing to the harvest, there will be no interruption of labour and no time for rest. And besides mowing, each has some other business to do—to plough up new land, and to harrow it; the women have cloth to make, bread to bake, and the washing to do; and the peasants must drive to the mill and to market; they have the official affairs of their community to attend to; they have also to provide the local government officials with means of locomotion, and to pass the night in the fields with the pastured horses. All, old and young and sick, work with all their strength. The peasants work in such a way that, when cutting the last rows, the mowers, weak people, growing youths, old men, are so tired that, having rested a little, it is with great pain they begin anew; the women, often with child, work hard too. It is a strained, incessant labour. . . . There is a small company labouring in the hayfield—three peasants—one of them an old man; another his nephew, who is married; and the third, the village bootmaker, a thin, wiry man, with their women, including one of about eighty, helping. They all draw up in line and work from morning to eve under the burning sun of June.

Let us turn to the country house. In the evening, when the rattle of the scythes of the returning toil-worn mowers, and the sounds of hammer and anvil are heard, there blend other sounds from the country house. Drin, drin, drin! goes the piano; a Hungarian song is heard through the noise of the croquet balls; before the stable an open carriage is standing, harnessed with four fat horses, which has been hired for twenty shillings to bring some guests a distance of ten miles. Horses standing by the carriage rattle their little bells. Before them hay has been thrown, which they are scattering with their hoofs, the same hay which the peasants have been gathering with such hard labour. In the yard of this mansion there is movement; a healthy, well-fed fellow in a pink shirt, presented to him for his service as a house-porter, is calling the coachmen, and telling them to harness and saddle some horses. Two peasants, who live here as coachmen, come out of their room, and go in an easy manner, swinging their arms, to saddle horses for the ladies and gentlemen. Still nearer to the house the sounds of another piano are heard. It is the music-mistress, who lives in the family to teach the children, practising her Schumann. The sounds of one piano jangle with those of another. Quite near the house walk two nurses; one is young, another old; they lead and carry children to bed; these children are of the same age as those who ran from the village with jugs. One nurse is English : she cannot speak Russian. She was engaged to come from England, not from being distinguished by some peculiar qualities, but simply because she does not speak Russian. Farther on is another person, a French woman, who is also engaged because she does not know Russian. Farther on a peasant, with two women, is watering flowers near the house ; another is cleaning a gun for one of the young gentlemen. Here two women are carrying a basket with clean linen—they have been washing for all these gentlefolks. In the house two women have scarcely time to wash the plates and dishes after the company, who have just done eating ; and two peasants in evening clothes are running up and down the stairs, serving coffee, tea, wine, seltzer-water, etc. Upstairs a table is spread. A meal has just ended; and another will soon begin, to continue till cock-crow, and often till morning dawns. Some are sitting smoking, playing cards; others are sitting and smoking, engaged in discoursing liberal ideas of reform ; and others, again, walk to and fro, eat, smoke, and, not knowing what to do, have made up their mind to take a drive. The household consists of fifteen persons, healthy men and women ; and thirty persons, healthy working people, male and female, labour for them. And this takes place there, where every hour, and each little boy, are precious, when the peasants, not having had their sleep out, will mow the oats at night, in order that it may not be lost, and the women will get up before dawn in order to finish their threshing in time. There will be private theatricals, picnics, hunting, drinking, eating, piano-playing, singing, dancing—in fact, incessant orgies. Yet we wonder at the inhumanity of a heartless Lucullus, who gorged himself with fine dishes and delicious wines while people were starving, and shake our heads over the barbarism and inhumanity of our grandfathers, the serf-owners.—*What then is to be Done?*

Men of science are so sure that this 'culture' is the greatest of blessings, that they boldly proclaim the contrary of what the jurists once said: *fiat justitia, pereat mundus.* They now say: *fiat cultura, pereat justitia.* Electric lights and telephones and exhibitions are excellent, and so are all the pleasure-gardens with concerts and performances, and all the cigars, and match-boxes, and braces, and motor-cars—but may they all go to perdition, and not they alone, but the railways, and all the factory-made chintz-stuffs and cloths in the world, if to produce them it is necessary that ninety-nine per cent. of the people should remain in slavery, and perish by thousands in factories needed for the production of these articles. Truly enlightened people will always agree to go back to riding on horses and using pack-horses, or even to tilling the earth with sticks and with their own hands, rather than to travel on railways which regularly every year crush a number of people, as is done in Chicago, merely because the proprietors of the railway find it more profitable to compensate the families of those killed than to build the line so that it should not kill people. The motto for truly enlightened people is not *fiat cultura, pereat justitia,* but *fiat justitia, pereat*

cultura. But true culture need not be destroyed.—
The Slavery of Our Times.

The Government and the Zemstvos, forsooth, have undertaken to spoon-feed the people! Now, who are they who take upon themselves to perform the task, and who is it that they thus take under their protecting wing? We, the noble-born tchinovniks of the Russian Empire, moved by a sentiment of charity and philanthropy, intend to feed our bread-winner, who himself feeds us all! The babe in arms will good-naturedly suckle its nurse, the parasite supply nutriment to the plant on which it lives and flourishes! We, the privileged classes, who fatten on the earnings of the horny-handed people, we who cannot move hand or foot without their aid, turn round and propose to feed them! In the very proposal, as it stands, there is something ludicrously strange, inconceivably grotesque. . . . The people are hungry and exhausted, and we, the upper classes, are very much concerned thereat, and would gladly stretch out a helping hand to rescue them. With this object we appoint committees, take an active part in their sittings, collect and subscribe money, purchase corn and distribute it to the destitute. But why are the people hungry? . . . It is a melancholy but undeniable fact that the entire agricultural population of Russia is systematically drugged with vodka, and cruelly sweated by merchants and tradesmen—and all for their own selfish, narrow ends. The result is writ large in the physical degeneration of the people and the alarming death-rate of children; men and women are rendered weak, will-less, shattered invalids, and children are killed off by the thousand, in order to enable our capitalists, aristocrats, and merchants to possess themselves of the wherewithal

I

to repose in the lap of luxury, to continue to lead the lives of sybarites in their sumptuous palaces, gorging themselves at Lucullan banquets, drinking the sounds of soft, sweet music at concerts and operas, listening to science distilled into popular lectures, etc. Why deceive ourselves? We want and care for the people only as instruments, as stepping-stones to our various goals of the moment; and, much as we desire to lay the flattering unction to our souls that we regard and treat them as members of the same family as ourselves, as men and as brothers, it is a fact that our interests are diametrically opposed to, and incompatible with, theirs, and that what is meat to us is rank poison and death to them.—*The Famine in Russia.*

III.—SOME PROPOSED REMEDIES

The cause of the miserable position of the workers cannot be found in the seizure of the means of production by capitalists. The cause must lie in that which drives them from the villages. And the emancipation of the workers from this state of things (even in that distant future in which science promises them liberty) can be accomplished neither by shortening the hours of labour, nor by increasing wages, nor by the promised communalisation of the means of production. All this cannot improve their position. For the labourers' misery consists not in the longer or shorter hours of work (agriculturists sometimes work eighteen hours a day, and as much as thirty-six hours on end, and consider their lives happy ones); nor does it consist in the low rate of wages, nor in the fact that the railway or the factory is not theirs; but it consists in the fact that they are obliged to work in harmful, unnatural conditions, often dangerous and

SOME PROPOSED REMEDIES

destructive to life, and to live a barrack life in towns—a life full of temptations and immorality—and to do compulsory labour at another's bidding. . . . Everywhere, notwithstanding the diminution of the hours of labour and the increase of wages, the health of the operatives is worse than that of country workers, the average duration of life is shorter, and morality is sacrificed, as cannot but occur when people are torn from those conditions which most conduce to morality: family life, and free, healthy, varied and intelligible agricultural work.

Economic science is so sure that all the peasants have inevitably to become factory operatives in towns that, though all the sages and the poets of the world have always placed the ideal of human happiness amid conditions of agricultural work—though all the workers whose habits are unperverted have always preferred, and still prefer, agricultural labour to any other—though factory work is always unhealthy and monotonous, while agriculture is most healthy and varied; while factory work, even if the factory belongs to the workmen, is always enforced, in dependence on the machines—though factory work is derivative, while agricultural work is fundamental, and without it no factory could exist—yet economic science affirms that all the country people not only are not injured by the transition from the country to the town, but themselves desire it, and strive towards it. The cause of this evidently unjust assertion is that those who have formulated, and who are formulating, the laws of science, belong to the well-to-do classes, and are so accustomed to the conditions, advantageous to themselves, in which they live, that they do not admit the thought that society could exist under other conditions.

The Socialist ideal is that the workers, having become masters of all the means of production, are to obtain all the comforts and pleasures now possessed by well-to-do people. They will all be well clothed and housed, and well nourished, and will all walk on electrically-lighted asphalt streets, and frequent concerts and theatres, and read papers and books, and ride on auto-cars, etc. But that everybody may have certain things, the production of those things must be apportioned, and consequently it must be decided how long each workman is to work. How is that to be decided? No statistics can show how much is wanted, and what articles are needed to satisfy the demand in a society where the means of production will belong to the society itself, *i.e.*, where the people will be free.... Furthermore, how are people to be induced to work at articles which some consider necessary and others consider unnecessary or even harmful? There will always be people who consider that, besides cannon and scents and whisky, exhibitions, academies, beer and beef are unnecessary and even harmful. How are these people to be made to participate in the production of such articles?... Some people will decide these questions and others will obey them.... Such division of labour as now exists will evidently be impossible in a free society.—*The Slavery of Our Times.*

Looking Backward is excellent. One thing is bad, namely, the Socialist, Marxian idea that if one does wrong for a very long time, good will ensue of its own accord. 'Capital is accumulated in the hands of a few; it will end by being held by one. All trades unions will be also united into one. There are capital and labour —divided. Authority or revolution will unite them, and all will be well.' The chief point is that nothing in our

SOME PROPOSED REMEDIES 133

civilisation will diminish, nothing recede; there will be the same mansions, the same gastronomic dinners, sweets, wines, carriages, horses, only everything will be accessible to all.

Individual labour is unprofitable; centralised labour is more profitable, but the inequality and oppression are terrible. Socialists wish to remove inequality and oppression by assigning all capital to the nation, to humanity, so that the centralised unit will become humanity itself. But among men striving each for his own welfare it would be impossible to find men sufficiently disinterested to manage the capital of humanity without taking advantage of their power—men who would not again introduce into the world inequality and oppression. . . . Some will say, 'Choose men who are wise and pure.' But none but the wise and pure can choose the wise and pure. And if all men were wise and pure, there would be no need of any organisation, consequently the impossibility of that which the revolutionary Socialists profess is felt by all, even by themselves; and that is why it is out of date and has no success. . . . However much advantages may increase, those who are at the top will appropriate them for themselves. . . . Wealth will all go to the men in authority as long as authority exists.—*Some Social Remedies.*

Humanity advances continually towards the enlightenment of its consciousness, and to the institution of modes of life corresponding to this consciousness. Hence in every period of life and humanity there is, on the one hand, a progressive enlightenment of consciousness, and, on the other, a realisation in life of what is enlightened. . . . At the present day a progressive enlightenment of human consciousness is taking place with reference to the use of land, and soon, it seems to me, a progressive realisation of this must follow. And in this progressive enlightenment with reference to the use of land, and its realisation, which constitutes one of the chief problems of our time, the fore-man, the leader of the movement, was and is Henry George. . . . It is Henry George's merit that he not only exploded all the sophism whereby religion and science justify landed property, and pressed the question to the farthest proof, which forced all who had not stopped their ears to acknowledge the unlawfulness of ownerships in land, but also that he was the first to indicate a possibility of solution for the question. He was the first to give a simple, straightforward answer to the usual excuses made by the enemies of all progress, which affirm that the demands of progress are illusions, impracticable, inapplicable. The method of Henry George destroys this excuse by so putting the question that by to-morrow committees might be appointed to examine and deliberate on his scheme and its transformation into law. In Russia, for instance, the inquiry as to the means for the ransom of land, or its gratuitous confiscation for nationalisation, might be begun to-morrow, and solved, with certain restrictions, as thirty-three years ago the question of liberating the peasants was solved. To humanity the indispensableness of this reform is demonstrated, and its feasibleness is proved (emendations, alterations in the single tax system may be required, but the fundamental idea is a possibility); and therefore humanity cannot but do that which their reason demands.—*Some Social Remedies.*

When I was a child I was told that if I wished to catch a bird I must put salt on its tail. I took a handful

SOME PROPOSED REMEDIES 135

and went in pursuit of the birds, but I saw at once that if I could sprinkle salt on their tails I could catch them, and that what I had been told was only a joke. Those who read essays and works on Courts of Arbitration and the disarmament of nations must feel very much the same. . . . History, however, shows us that the governments, as seen from the reign of Cæsar to those of the two Napoleons and Prince Bismarck, are in their very essence a violation of justice; a man or a body of men having at command an army of trained soldiers, deluded creatures who are ready for any violence, and through whose agency they govern the State, will have no keen sense of the obligation of justice. Therefore, governments will never consent to diminish the number of those well-trained and submissive servants who constitute their power and influence. . . . And there really are men who spend their time in promoting Leagues of Peace, in delivering addresses, and in writing books; and of course the governments sympathise with it all, pretending that they approve of it, just as they pretend to support temperance, while they actually derive the larger part of their income from intemperance; just as they pretend to maintain liberty of the constitution, when it is the absence of liberty to which they owe their power; just as they pretend to care for the improvement of the labouring classes, while on oppression of the workmen rest the very foundations of the State; just as they pretend to uphold Christianity when Christianity is subversive of every government.— *The Kingdom of God is Within You.*

It is said that the conflicts between Governments are to be decided by arbitration. But, apart from the fact that the disputes will be settled, not by representatives of the people, but by representatives of the Governments, and that there is no guarantee that the decisions will be just ones, who is to carry out the decisions of the court? The army? ... The arbitrator's sentence against the military violence of States will be carried out by military violence—that is to say, the thing that has to be checked is to be the instrument by which it is to be checked. To catch a bird, put salt on its tail!

For international questions to be decided by courts of arbitration there must be, among the Powers, full mutual confidence that the decisions of the court will be respected. If there is such confidence, no armies are necessary. But if armies exist, it is obvious that this confidence is lacking, and that international questions can be decided only by the strength of the armies.

The Governments wish to persuade the peoples that there is no need for private individuals to trouble about freeing themselves from wars; the Governments themselves, at their conferences, will arrange first to reduce and presently quite to abolish armies. But this is untrue. Armies can be reduced and abolished only in opposition to the will, but never by the will, of Governments. Armies will only be diminished and abolished when people cease to trust Governments, and themselves seek salvation from the miseries that oppress them, and seek that safety, not by the complicated and delicate combinations of diplomatists, but in the simple fulfilment of that law, binding upon every man, inscribed in all religious teachings, and present in every heart, not to do to others what you wish them not to do to you— above all, not to slay your neighbours.—*The Peace Conference.*

The so-called question of woman's rights arose, and only could arise, among men who had deviated from the law of real labour. One has only to return to it, and that question must cease to exist. A woman who has her own particular, inevitable labour will never claim the right of sharing man's labour — in mines, or in ploughing fields. She claims a share only in the sham labour of the wealthy classes.

The means of serving others are various for men. The whole activity of mankind, with the exception of bearing children and rearing them, is open for his service to men. A woman, in addition to the possibility of serving men by all the means open to man, by the construction of her body is called, and is inevitably attracted, to serve others by that which alone is excepted from the domain of the service of man. The service of mankind is divided into two parts—one, the augmentation of the welfare of mankind; the other, the continuation of the race. Men are called chiefly to the first, as they are deprived of the possibility of fulfilling the second. Women are called exclusively to the second, as they only are fitted for it. This difference one should not, one can not, forget or destroy; and it would be sinful to do so. From this difference proceed the duties of each—duties not invented by men, but which are in the nature of things.

The vocation of man is broader and more varied; the vocation of woman more uniform and narrower, but more profound. And therefore it has always been and always will be the case that man, having hundreds of duties, will be neither a bad nor a pernicious man, even when he has been false to one or ten out of them, if he fulfils the greater part of his vocation; while woman, as she has a smaller number of duties, if she is false to one of them, instantly falls lower than a man who has been false to ten out of his hundreds of duties. Such has always been the general opinion, and such it will always remain—because such is the substance of the matter. . . . In the general vocation of serving God and others, man and woman are entirely equal, notwithstanding the difference of the form of that service. The equality consists in the equal importance of one service and of the other—that the one is impossible without the other, that the one depends upon the other, and that for efficient service, as well for man as for woman, the knowledge of truth is equally necessary.

The ideal woman, in my opinion, is one who, appropriating the highest view of life of the time in which she lives, yet gives herself to her feminine mission, which is irresistibly placed in her—that of bringing forth, nursing and educating the greatest possible number of children, fitted to work for people according to the view which she has of life. But in order to appropriate the highest view of life, I think there is no need of attending lectures; all that she requires is to read the gospel, and not to shut her eyes, ears, and, most of all, her heart. Well, and if you ask what those are to do who have no children, who are not married, or are widows, I answer that those will do well to share man's multifarious labour. But one cannot help being sorry that such a precious tool as woman is should be bereft of the possibility of fulfilling the great vocation which it is proper to her alone to fulfil.—*What then is to be Done?*

CHAPTER III

THE GREAT COMMANDMENTS

I.—THE LAW OF REASON

To those who ask my opinion whether it be desirable to endeavour by the aid of reason to attain complete consciousness in one's inner spiritual life, and to express the truths thus attained in definite language, I would answer in the positive affirmative, that every man to achieve his destiny on earth and to attain true welfare—the two are synonymous—must continually exert all his mental faculties to solve for himself and clearly to express the religious foundations on which he lives—that is, the meaning of his life. I have often found among illiterate labourers, who have to deal with cubic measurements, an accepted conviction that mathematical calculations are fallacious, and not to be trusted. . . . A similar opinion has obtained among men who, I will boldly say, are bereft of true religious feelings, that reason is unequal to the solution of religious questions, that the application of reason to such questions is the most fruitful source of error, and that the solution of such questions by the aid of reason is sinful pride. . . . Man has been given by God one single instrument to attain knowledge of self, and of one's relation to the universe: there is no other—and that one is reason. . . . Man cannot be conscious of anything independently of reason. It is said, Accept the truth by revelation, by faith. But a man cannot believe independently of reason. If a man believes this and not that, it is only because his reason tells him that this is credible and that is not.—*Demands of Love and Reason.*

The law which men should follow is so plain that it is accessible to every child, the more so as no man has to discover anew the law of his life. Those who have lived before him have discovered and expressed it, and he has but to verify it with his reason, and to accept or refuse those propositions which he finds expressed in tradition. . . . Traditions may proceed from men and be false, but reason indubitably comes from God, and cannot be false. Particular intellectual qualities are needful, not for the acquirement and expression of truth, but for the concoction and expression of error. . . . A righteous God has created evil, persecutes men, demands redemption, and so forth; and we, professing the law of love and mercy, execute, make war, rob the poor, etc. To disentangle these impossible contradictions, or rather to conceal them from oneself, much mental capacity and special talent are indeed necessary; but to learn the law of one's life, or, as already expressed, to bring one's faith into complete consciousness, no special mental capacity is required; one has but to refuse to admit anything contrary to reason, not to deny reason, religiously to guard one's reason and to rely on it alone.

According to the doctrine of Christ, a man who limits his observation of life to the sphere in which there is no freedom—to the sphere of effects, that is, of acts—does not live a true life. He only lives a true life who has transferred his life into the sphere where freedom lives—

into the domain of first causes—by the recognition and practice of the truth revealed to him. He thus unites himself with the source of universal life and accomplishes not personal, individual acts that depend on conditions of time and space, but acts that have no causes, but are in themselves causes of all else and have an endless and unlimited significance. . . . Men have but to understand this: that they must cease to care for material and external matters, in which they are not free; let them apply one-hundredth part of the energy now used by them in outward concerns to those in which they are free—to the recognition and profession of the truth that confronts them, to the deliverance of themselves and others from the falsehood and hypocrisy which conceal the truth—and then the false system of life which now torments us, which threatens us with still greater suffering, will be destroyed at once without struggle. Then the Kingdom of Heaven, at least in that first stage for which men through the development of their consciousness are already prepared, will be established. As one shake is sufficient to precipitate into crystals a liquid saturated with salt, so at the present time it may be that only the least effort is needed in order that the truth already revealed to us should spread among hundreds, thousands, millions of men, and a public opinion become established in conformity with the existing consciousness, and the entire social organisation become transformed. It depends upon us to make this effort.—*The Kingdom of God is Within You.*

The ideal is to take no thought for the morrow, to live in the present; and the commandment the fulfilment of which is the point beneath which we must not fall is against taking oaths or making promises for the future.

In order to free himself from religious deception in general, man must understand and remember that the only instrument he possesses for the acquisition of knowledge is reason, and therefore that every teaching affirming what is contrary to reason is a delusion, an attempt to set aside the only instrument for acquiring knowledge which God has given to man. Man can receive truth only through his reason. The man, therefore, who thinks that he receives truth through faith and not through reason only deludes himself and uses his reason for a purpose for which it was never intended—namely, to solve questions as to which of those who transmit what is given out as truth must be believed, and which rejected. Whereas reason is intended, not to decide between whom one must and must not believe (this, indeed, it cannot do), but to verify the truth of what is presented to it. This it can always do; for this purpose it was designed.

Misinterpreters of truth generally say that one cannot trust reason because its assertions vary in different men, and that it is therefore better, for the sake of union, to believe in revelation confirmed by miracles. But they make a mistake, and, intentionally or unintentionally, confuse reason with speculation and invention. Speculations and inventions, it is true, may be, and are, infinitely diverse and numerous, but the conclusions of reason are the same for all men at all times. . . . Therefore, to avoid falling a prey to religious deception, man must understand and remember that truth is revealed to him only through reason, given him by God for the purpose of discovering the will of God, and that the practice of inspiring distrust in reason is founded on the desire to deceive, and is the greatest blasphemy.—*The Christian Teaching.*

II.—Law of Peace, or Non-Resistance by Force

The ideal is to bear no malice, excite no ill-will, and to love all men. The commandment which forbids us to offend our neighbour is one which a man who is striving to attain this ideal must not do less than obey. And this is the first commandment. The ideal—to use no violence whatsoever—shows that we must return good for evil, endure injuries with patience, and give up the cloak to him who has taken the coat. The ideal is to love your enemies, to do good to them that despitefully use you. In order to keep the spirit of this commandment, one must at least refrain from injuring one's enemies, one must speak kindly of them, and treat all one's fellow-creatures with equal consideration. All these commandments are reminders of that which we, in our striving for perfection, must and can avoid; reminders, too, that we must labour now to acquire by degrees habits of self-restraint, until such habits become second nature. But these commandments, far from exhausting the doctrine, do not by any means cover it. They are but stepping-stones on the way to perfection, and must necessarily be followed by higher and still higher ones, as men pursue the course towards perfection. That is why a Christian doctrine would make higher demands than those embodied in the commandments, and not in the least decrease its demands, as they who judge the Christian doctrine from a social life-conception seem to think.—*The Kingdom of God.*

The reply to the question, What must we do? is very simple, and not merely definite, but always in the highest degree applicable and practicable for each man . . . for it demands the activity of that one person over whom each of us has real, rightful, and unquestionable power, namely, oneself; and it consists in this, that if a man— whether slave or slave-owner—really wishes to better not *his* position alone, but the position of people in general, he must not himself do those wrong things which enslave him and his brothers. And in order not to do the evil which produces misery for himself and his brothers, *he should, first of all, neither willingly, nor under compulsion, take any part in Governmental activity, and should therefore be neither a soldier, nor a Field-Marshal, nor a Member of State, nor a tax-collector, nor a witness, nor an alderman, nor a juryman, nor a governor, nor a Member of Parliament, nor, in fact, hold any office connected with violence.* That is one thing.

Secondly, *such a man should not voluntarily pay taxes to Governments, either directly or indirectly; nor should he accept money collected by taxes, either as salary, or as pension, or as a reward, nor should he make use of Governmental institutions supported by taxes collected by violence from the people.* That is the second thing.

Thirdly, *a man who desires not to promote his own well-being alone, but to better the position of people in general, should not appeal to Governmental violence for the protection of his possessions in land or in other things, nor to defend him and his near ones; but should only possess land and all products of his own and the people's toil in so far as others do not claim them from him.*—The Slavery of Our Times.

The willing acceptance of a condition by men is the sole criterion of its good. And the lives of men abound with such acts. . . . . Roads, churches, and museums, and various social and state affairs may be good for those who consider it good, and who therefore freely and willingly perform it. But the work to which men must be driven by force ceases to be a common good precisely by the fact of such violence.—*What then is to be Done?*

The cruellest of snares—that of the State—is, like false religion, transmitted to men by two modes of deception —inculcation of falsehood into children, and influence exerted on the feelings of men by external solemnities. On awakening to consciousness, almost every man who lives in a State finds himself already entangled in State snares, and living under the persuasion that his is a superior, special people, State, country, for the welfare and advancement of which he should blindly obey the existing Government, and at its bidding torture, wound, and slay his fellows. The evil of this snare is that, as soon as we admit the possibility of ascertaining and understanding what constitutes the welfare of a number of people, there is no limit to conjecture as to the resultant welfare from any act whatever; so that any act may be justified the moment a man assumes that the welfare or life of one man may be sacrificed for the sake of the future welfare of many. There is no limit to the evil that can be done in the name of such reasoning. The first assumption—that we can know what will promote the future welfare of many—has been responsible in former times for torture, the Inquisition, and slavery, and, in our time, for courts of law, prisons, and landed property. Acting on the second assumption—that of Caiaphas—Christ was slain in the past, and at the present time millions perish by executions and war.

In order to avoid falling into this snare man must understand and remember that before belonging to any

State or nation he belongs to God, being a member of a universal kingdom, and that so far from being able to transfer to anyone the responsibility for his actions, he must himself alone always be answerable for them. Therefore, man must under no circumstances prefer men of his own nation or State to those of another; no consideration as to the future welfare of many must ever induce him to do harm to his neighbours; and he must not think that he ought to obey anyone whatever in preference to his own conscience.—*The Christian Teaching.*

The first criticisms [of 'My Religion'] with which I deal came mostly from men of high position, either in Church or State, who feel quite sure that no one will venture to combat their assertions, and have forgotten that there is a Christianity in whose name they hold their places. They condemn as sectarian all that which is Christ-like in Christianity . . . and to show that it is not opposed to violence quote equivocal passages from the Old and New Testaments, and all of Christ's words that can possibly be misinterpreted—the expulsion from the Temple and other passages. Such men turn away from Christ Himself, to invent an ideal and a form of religion all their own, forgetful of Him in whose name both the Church and the offices they hold exist. If men but knew that the Church preaches an unforgiving, murder-loving, and belligerent Christ, they would not believe in that Church, and its doctrines would be defended by none.

The second method, somewhat more awkward, consists in affirming that though Christ did, in point of fact, teach us to turn the other cheek, and to share our cloak, and that these are indeed lofty moral laws, still . . .

the world abounds in evil-doers, and if these wretches are not subdued by force, the righteous will perish and the world will be destroyed. . . . This argument is groundless, because if we allow ourselves to look upon our fellow-men as evil-doers, outcasts (Rakà), we sap the very foundations of the Christian doctrine, which teaches us that we, the children of the Heavenly Father, are brothers and equal one to the other. In the second place, if the same Father had permitted us to use violence towards evil-doers, as there is no infallible rule for distinguishing the good from the evil, every individual or every community might class its neighbours under the head of evil-doers, which is practically the case at the present time.

Whether the tyranny of the State is or is not to be abolished, the position of the innocent who are oppressed by the tyrants will not be materially affected thereby. Men are not to be frightened by being told that the wicked will oppress the good, because that is the natural course and will never change. When the rulers say that if their power were to be destroyed the evil-doers would tyrannise over the innocent, what they really mean is that the tyrants in power are reluctant to yield to those other tyrants who would fain wrest from them their authority. . . . If State violence disappeared, it is not unlikely that other acts of violence would be committed; but the sum of violence can never be increased simply because the power passes from the hands of one into those of another.

The third and more ingenious reply is that while to obey the commandment of non-resistance is every Christian's duty when the injury is a personal one, it ceases to be obligatory when harm is done to one's neighbour, and that in such an emergency a Christian is bound to use force against the evil-doer. This assertion is purely arbitrary and finds no justification throughout the whole body of the teaching of Christ, and, in fact, amounts to a direct negative. How may we define what is called danger to one's neighbour? If my private judgment is to be the arbiter, any violence can be excused. Magicians have been burned, aristocrats and Girondists put to death, because the men in power considered them dangerous. If this important condition, which destroys the significance of the commandment, ever entered into the thought of Christ, it would have been formulated somewhere. Not only is no such exception to the commandment to be found throughout the Teacher's life and lessons, but there is on the other hand a warning against an interpretation so false and misleading, in the Bible story of Caiaphas, who admitted that it was not well to put to death the innocent Jesus, but perceived the existence of a danger, not for himself, but for all the people, and therefore declared it better for one man to die than for a whole nation to perish. And we have a still more explicit proof of the fallacy of this interpretation in the words addressed to Peter, when he tried to revenge by violence the attack upon Jesus (Matthew xxvi. 51). Peter was defending, not himself, but his beloved and divine Master, and Christ distinctly forbade him, saying, 'For all they that take the sword shall perish with the sword' (Matthew xxvi. 52). It is impossible to compare one act of violence with the other, and to say which is the greater, that which one is about to commit, or the wrong done against one's neighbour. We release society from the presence of a criminal by putting him to death, but we cannot possibly know that the former might not have so changed by the morrow as to render the execution a useless cruelty. We imprison another, we believe him a dangerous man, but no later than next day this very man may have ceased to be dangerous, and his imprisonment has become unnecessary. . . . What a vast amount of harm must and does accrue from the assurance that a man feels of his right to provide against a possible calamity. Ninety-nine parts of the world's iniquity, from the Inquisition to the bomb-throwing of the present day, and the execution of tens of thousands of political criminals, so called, result from this very assurance.

The fourth and still more ingenious reply consists in asserting that this commandment is not denied but acknowledged like all the others; it is only the special significance attributed to it by sectarians that is denied. . . . It has, they say, the importance, no more and no less, of all the others; and one who through weakness has transgressed against any of the commandments, whether that of non-resistance, or another, does not for that cause cease to be a Christian, provided his creed be true. . . . One has, however, but to compare the attitude of the clergy towards this or any of the other commandments which they do acknowledge, to be convinced that it is quite different from their attitude towards this one. The commandment against fornication they acknowledge without reservation, and in no case will they ever admit that this sin is not an evil. . . . Clergymen have never been known to advocate the breaking of any other commandment, but in regard to the teaching of non-resistance they distinctly teach that this prohibition must not be taken too literally, that so far from always obeying this commandment we should on occasion follow the opposite course—sit in judgment, go to war, execute criminals, etc. . . . How is this commandment to become less difficult when its infraction is not only condoned but directly encouraged?

The fifth method of answering, the most popular one of all, consists in quiet evasion, pretending that the question was solved ages ago, in a cogent and satisfactory manner, and that it would be a waste of words to re-open the subject. This method is employed by all the more cultured authors, who, if they made answer at all, would feel themselves bound to be logical. . . . As a characteristic specimen of these criticisms, I will quote from an article by that well-known and scholarly Englishman, the writer and preacher, Canon Farrar, who, like so many other learned theologians, is an expert in the art of silently ignoring and evading a statement. The article appeared in *The Forum* for October 1888. . . . Farrar expresses his belief that 'though actuated by the noblest sincerity, Count Tolstoy has been misled by partial and one-sided interpretations of the meaning of the Gospel and the mind and will of Christ.' In what this error consists he does not explain, but says: '*To enter into the proof of this is impossible in this article, for I have already exceeded the space at my command*,' and concludes with equanimity: 'Meanwhile the reader who feels troubled lest it should be his duty also to forsake all the conditions of his life, and to take up the position and work of a common labourer, may rest for the present on the principle, "securus judicat orbis terrarum." With few and rare exceptions the whole of Christendom, from the days of the apostles down to our own, has come to the firm conclusion that it was the object of Christ to lay down great eternal principles, but not to disturb the bases and revolutionise the institutions as well as all inevitable conditions. Were it my object to prove how untenable is the doctrine of Communism, based by Count Tolstoy upon the divine paradoxes, which can be interpreted on only historical principles in accordance with the whole method of the teaching of Jesus, it would require an ampler canvas than I have here at my disposal.' What a pity that he has no space! And, wonderful to relate, no one for fifteen centuries ever had the space to prove that the Christ whom we profess said one thing and meant another. And of course they could prove it if they would! But it is not worth while to prove what everybody knows to be true. It is enough to say: 'Securus judicat orbis terrarum.'—*The Kingdom of God is Within You.*

It is said that without Governments we should not have those institutions—enlightening, educational and public—that are needful for all. But why should we suppose this? We see, on the contrary, that in the most diverse matters people in our times arrange their own lives incomparably better than those who govern them arrange things for them. Without the least help from Government, and often in spite of the interference of Government, people organise all sorts of social undertakings—workmen's unions, co-operative societies, railway companies, *artéls* [associations of labourers in Russia], and syndicates. If collections for public works are needed, why should we suppose that free people could not, without violence, voluntarily collect the necessary means and carry out anything that is now carried out by means of taxes, if only the undertakings in question are really useful for everybody? Why suppose that there cannot be tribunals without violence?

Trial by people trusted by the disputants has always existed and will exist, and needs no violence. We are so depraved by long-continued slavery that we can hardly imagine administration without violence. And, yet again, that is not true: Russian communes migrating to distant regions, where our Government leaves them alone, arrange their own taxation, administration, tribunals, and police, and always prosper until governmental violence interferes with their administration. And in the same way there is no reason to suppose that people could not, by common agreement, decide how the land is to be apportioned for use.

Things really produced by a man's own labour, and that he needs, are always protected by custom, by public opinion, by feelings of justice and reciprocity, and they do not need to be protected by violence. . . . The defence by violence of the rights of property immorally obtained, which is now customary, if it has not quite destroyed, has considerably weakened people's natural consciousness of justice in the matter of using articles, *i.e.*, has weakened the natural and innate right of property, without which humanity could not exist, and which has always existed and still exists among all men. And, therefore, there is no reason to anticipate that people will not be able to arrange their lives without organised violence.—*The Slavery of Our Times.*

The question as put by Christ is not at all, Can non-resistance become a general law for humanity? but, How must each man act to fulfil his allotted task, to save his soul, and to do the will of God?—which are all really one and the same thing. Christian teaching does not lay down laws for everybody, and does not say to people,

'You, all, for fear of punishment, must obey such and such rules, and then you will all be happy'; but it explains to each individual his position in relation to the world, and lets him see what results, for him individually, inevitably flow from that relation.

To many people of our society it would be impossible to torture or kill a baby, even if they were told that by so doing they could save hundreds of other people. And in the same way a man, when he has developed a Christian sensibility of heart, finds a whole series of actions become impossible for him. For certain actions are morally impossible, just as others are physically impossible. As a man cannot lift a mountain, and as a kindly man cannot kill an infant, so a man living the Christian life cannot take part in deeds of violence.

How (to use the stock example) is a man to act when he sees a robber killing or outraging a child, and he can only save the child by killing the robber? When such a case is put, it is generally assumed that the only possible reply is that one should kill the robber to save the child. But this answer is given so quickly and decidedly only because we are all so accustomed to the use of violence. . . . By killing the robber he certainly kills, whereas he cannot know positively whether the robber would have killed the child or not. But letting that pass, who shall say whether the child's life was more needed, was better, than the robber's life? To decide that he needs to know what would become of the child whom he saves, and what—had he not killed him—would have been the future of the robber he kills. And as he cannot know this, the non-Christian has no sufficient rational ground for killing a robber to save a child. If a man is a Christian, and consequently acknowledges God and sees the meaning of life in fulfilling His will, then, however ferocious the robber, however innocent and lovely the child, he has even less ground to abandon the God-given law and to do to the robber what the robber wishes to do to the child. He may plead with the robber, may interpose his own body between the robber and the victim, but there is one thing he cannot do: he cannot deliberately abandon the law he has received from God, the fulfilment of which alone gives meaning to his life. Very probably bad education, or his animal nature, may cause a man (Christian or non-Christian) to kill the robber, not only to save the child, but even to save himself or to save his purse, but it does not follow that he is right in acting thus, or that he should accustom himself or others to think such conduct right.

I see a robber killing a child, and I can save the child by killing the robber—therefore in certain cases violence must be used to resist evil. A man's life is in danger, and can be saved only by my telling a lie—therefore in certain cases one must lie. A man is starving, and one can save him only by stealing—therefore in certain cases one must steal. . . .

'*Fais ce que tu dois, advienne que pourra*' ('Do what you ought, come what may') is an expression of profound wisdom. We each can know indubitably what we ought to do—but what results will follow from our actions we none of us either do know or can know. Therefore it follows that, besides feeling the call of duty, we are further driven to act as duty bids us by the consideration that we have no other guidance, but are totally ignorant of what will result from our actions. . . .

None of us has ever yet met the imaginary robber with the imaginary child, but all the horrors which fill the annals of history and of our own times came and come from this one thing—that people will believe that they can foresee the results of hypothetical future actions.

It was just this sophistical justification of violence that Christ denounced. When two enemies fight, each may think his own conduct justified by the circumstances. Excuses can be made for every use of violence; and no infallible standard has ever been discovered by which to measure the worth of these excuses. Therefore Christ taught not to believe in any excuse for violence, and (contrary to what had been taught by them of old time) never to use violence.—*Letters on the Personal Christian Life.*

The Anarchists are right in everything, in the negation of the existing order and in the assertion that, without authority, there could not be worse violence than that of authority under existing conditions. They are mistaken only in thinking that Anarchy can be instituted by a revolution. It will be instituted only by there being more and more people who do not require protection from governmental power and by there being more and more people who will be ashamed of applying this power.

Dynamite and the dagger, as experience has already shown, only cause reaction, and destroy the most valuable power, the only one at our command, that of public opinion. The alternative—to come to an agreement with the Government, making concessions to it, participating in it, in order gradually to disentangle the net which is binding the people, and to set them free—is closed, because governments have already learnt how far they may allow the participation of men wishing to reform them. They admit only that which does not infringe, which is non-essential; and they are very sensitive concerning things harmful to them—sensitive because the matter concerns their own existence. They admit men who do not share their views, and who desire reform, not only in order to satisfy the demands of these men, but also in their own interest, in that of the Government. . . . To join the ranks of the Government is also impossible—one would only become its instrument. One course, therefore, remains—to fight the Government by means of thought, speech, actions, life, neither yielding to Government nor joining its ranks and thereby increasing its power.

There can be only one permanent revolution—a moral one: the regeneration of the inner man.—*Some Social Remedies.*

If only the best and unfettered men, sincerely desirous of serving the people, could realise that it is not possible to improve, by any external means, the condition of a man who thinks it wrong to eat meat on Fridays, and right to punish by death a guilty individual, or one who thinks it important to render the necessary homage to an image or an emperor and non-important to swear obedience to the will of other men and to train oneself to murder! If only men would realise that neither parliaments, nor strikes, trade unions, nor co-operative societies, inventions, schools, universities and academies, nor revolutions, can be of any real use to men holding a false religious life-conception! If only this were understood, all the energies of the best men would be applied, not to the consequences, but to the cause; not to State activity, or revolution, or Socialism, but to the denunciation of the false religious doctrine, and the rebuilding of the true one.—*The Root of the Evil.*

Of what apparent importance are such acts as the refusal of a score or two of fools, as they are called, to take the oath of allegiance, to pay taxes, or to take part in courts of law, or to serve in the army? Such men are tried and condemned, and life remains unchanged. These occurrences may seem unimportant, and yet these are precisely the factors that undermine the authority of the Government more than any others, and thus prepare the way for the liberation of mankind. These are the bees who are the first to separate themselves from the swarm, and still hovering near, they wait for the whole swarm to rise and follow them. The governments are aware of this, and look upon such occurrences with more apprehension than upon all the Socialists, Anarchists, and Communists, with their conspiracies and their dynamite bombs.

Such instances of a refusal to comply with the demands of the State when opposed to Christianity, especially refusals to perform military service, occur not only in Russia but everywhere, and become more numerous. . . . What can be done with men who wish neither to destroy nor to establish anything, whose sole desire is to avoid in their own private lives any act that may be opposed to the Christian law, and who consequently refuse to perform duties which are regarded by the Government as the most natural and obligatory of all? . . . They cannot be bribed or deceived or intimidated.

... Neither can they be executed or imprisoned for life. Their past lives, their thoughts and actions, their friends, speak for them; everyone knows them to be gentle, kindly, and harmless men, and it is impossible to represent them in the light of criminals. ... Confronted with these insubordinations, governments find themselves in a desperate plight. They realise that the prophecies of Christianity are about to be fulfilled, that it is loosening the fetters of them that are in bonds and setting men free; they realise that such freedom will inevitably destroy those who have held mankind in bondage. Governments realise this; they know that their hours are counted, that they are helpless to resist. —*The Kingdom of God is Within You.*

The abolition of governments will merely rid us of an unnecessary organisation which we have inherited from the past for the commission of violence and for its justification. 'But there will then be no laws, no property, no courts of justice, no police, no popular education,' say people who intentionally confuse the use of violence by governments with various social activities. The abolition of the organisation of government formed to do violence does not at all involve the abolition of what is reasonable and good, and therefore not based on violence, in laws or law courts, or in property, or in police regulations, or in financial arrangements, or in popular education. On the contrary, the absence of the brutal power of government, which is needed only for its own support, will facilitate a more just and reasonable social organisation, needing no violence. Courts of justice, and public affairs, and popular education, will all exist to the extent to which they are really needed by the people, but in a shape which will not involve the evils contained in the present form of government. What will be destroyed is merely what was evil and hindered the free expression of the people's will.

Understand that salvation from your woes is only possible when you free yourself from the obsolete idea of patriotism and from the obedience to governments that is based upon it, and when you boldly enter into the region of that higher idea, the brotherly union of the peoples, which has long since come to life, and from all sides is calling you to itself.—*Patriotism and Government.*

'All this comes,' Nekhlúdoff thought, 'from the fact that these people, governors, inspectors, police officers and policemen, consider that there are circumstances when human relations are not necessary between human beings. If anything be accepted as more important than the feeling of love for one's fellow-men, though it be but for a single hour, or only in some exceptional case, there will then be no crime that may not be committed without the perpetrators feeling themselves guilty. . . . I am simply afraid of these people, and really they are terrible, more terrible than robbers. A robber might, after all, feel pity, but they can feel no pity, they are inured against pity as these stones are against vegetation. That is what makes them terrible. If a psychological problem were set to find means of making men of our time—Christian, humane, simple, kind people—perform the most horrible crimes without feeling guilty, only one solution could be devised : to go on doing what is being done. It is only necessary that these people should be governors, inspectors, policemen; that they should be fully convinced that there is a kind of business called

Government service, which allows men to treat other men as things, without having human brotherly relations with them; and also that these people should be so linked together by this Government service that the responsibility for the results of their actions should not fall on any one of them separately. Without these conditions the terrible acts I witnessed to-day would be impossible in our times.'

' It all lies in the fact that men think there are circumstances when one may deal with human beings without love; and there are no such circumstances. You may deal with things without love; you may cut down trees, make bricks, hammer iron without love, but you cannot deal with men without it, just as you cannot deal with bees without being careful. . . . If you feel no love, sit still,' Nekhlúdoff thought; 'occupy yourself with things, with yourself, with anything you like, only not with men.'

It happened to Nekhlúdoff as it often happens to men who are living a spiritual life. The thought that seemed strange at first and paradoxical, or even to be only a joke, being confirmed more and more often by life's experience, suddenly appeared as the simplest, truest certainty. In this way the idea that the only certain means of salvation from the terrible evil from which men are suffering is that they should always acknowledge themselves to be sinning against God, and therefore unable to punish or correct others, became clear to him. It became clear to him that all the dreadful evil he had been witnessing in prisons and jails, and the quiet self-satisfaction of the perpetrators of this evil, were the consequences of men trying to do what was impossible; trying to correct evil while being evil themselves; vicious men were trying to correct other vicious men, and thought they could do it by using mechanical means. And the result of all this is that the needs and cupidity of some men induce them to take up this so-called punishment and correction as a profession, and they themselves become utterly corrupt, and go on unceasingly depraving those whom they torment. Now he saw clearly whence came all the horrors he had seen, and what ought to be done to put a stop to them. The answer he had been unable to find was the same that Christ gave to Peter. It was that we should forgive always an infinite number of times, because there are no men who have not themselves sinned, and therefore no one can punish or correct others.—*Resurrection*.

III.—THE LAW OF LABOUR.

To the question, 'What is to be done?' I answer first of all that we must neither deceive other men nor ourselves; that we must not be afraid of the truth whatever the result may be. . . . We, not only rich men but men in a privileged position, so-called educated men, have gone so far astray that we require either a firm resolution or very great sufferings on our false way in order to come to our senses again, and to recognise the lie by which we live. . . . The second answer to the question, resulting from the first, consisted for me in repenting, in the full meaning of this word, that is, entirely changing the estimate of my own position and activity. Instead of considering that position to be useful and of importance, we must come to acknowledge it to be harmful and trifling; instead of considering ourselves educated, we must get to see our ignorance;

instead of imagining ourselves to be kind and moral, we must acknowledge that we are immoral and cruel; instead of our importance, we must see our own insignificance. . . . If the question had been put after I had repented, 'What have I, so ruined a man, to do?' the answer would have been easy: First of all, I must try to get my living honestly—that is, learn not to live upon the shoulders of others; and while learning this, and after I have learned it, to try on every occasion to be of use to men with my hands and with my feet, as well as with my brain and heart, and with all of me that is wanted by man. . . . My first and unquestionable business is to earn my living, clothing, heating, building, and so forth, and in doing this to serve others as well as myself. Every other activity of man is only lawful when these first have been satisfied.

It became undoubtedly certain to me that just as all those inventions of the human mind, such as newspapers, theatres, concerts, parties, balls, cards, magazines, novels, are nothing else than means to sustain the mental life of men out of its natural condition of labour for others, in the same way all the hygienic and medical inventions of the human mind for their accommodation, food, drink, dwelling, ventilation, warming of rooms, clothes, medicines, mineral waters, gymnastics, electric and other cures, are all merely means to sustain the bodily life of man out of its natural conditions of labour; that all these are nothing else than an establishment hermetically closed, in which, by the means of chemical apparatus, the evaporation of water for the plants is arranged, when you only need to open the window, and do that which is natural, not only to men but to beasts too; in other words, having absorbed the food, and thus produced a charge of energy, to discharge it by muscular labour. All the profound thoughts of hygiene and of the art of healing for the men of our circle are like the efforts of a mechanic who, having stopped all the valves of an overheated engine, should invent something to prevent this engine from bursting.

I picture to myself the whole matter thus: Every man's day is divided by his meals into four parts, or four stages as they are called by the peasants: First, before breakfast; secondly, from breakfast to dinner; thirdly, from dinner to poldnik (a slight evening meal between dinner and supper); and fourthly, from poldnik to night. The activity of man to which he is drawn is also divided into four kinds: First, the activity of the muscles, the labour of the hands, feet, shoulders, back—hard labour by which one perspires; secondly, the activity of the fingers and wrists, the activity of skill and handicraft; thirdly, the activity of the intellect and imagination; fourthly, the activity of intercourse with other men. . . . And the goods which man makes use of may also be divided into four kinds: First, every man makes use of the productions of hard labour—bread, cattle, buildings, wells, bridges, and so on; secondly, the productions of handicraft—clothes, boots, hardware, and so on; thirdly, the productions of mental activity—science, art; and fourthly, the intercourse with men—acquaintanceship, societies. And I thought that it would be the best thing so to arrange the occupations of the day that one might be able to exercise all these four faculties, and to return all the four kinds of production of labour which one makes use of, so that the four parts of the day were devoted, first, to hard labour; secondly, to mental labour; thirdly, to handicraft; fourthly, to the intercourse with men. It would be good if one could so arrange his labour; but if it is not possible to arrange thus, one thing is important—to acknowledge the duty of labouring, the duty of making a good use of each part of the day.

For men who consider labour to be the essential thing and the joy of life, the ground, the basis of it will always be the struggle with nature—not only agricultural labour, but also that of handicraft, mental work, and intercourse with men. The divergence from one or many of these kinds of labour, and specialties of labour, will be performed only when a man of special gifts, being fond of this work, and knowing that he performs it better than anybody else, will sacrifice his own advantage in order to fulfil the demands of others put directly to him. Only with such a view of labour, and the natural division of labour resulting from it, will the curse disappear which we in our imagination have put upon labour, and every labour will always be a joy.—*What then is to be Done?*

The fundamental idea of Bondareff's work, *The Triumph of the Labourer*, may be given thus—In all practical affairs the important question is, not what is good and should be known, but, of all good things and needful knowledge, what is of primary importance, what of secondary, and so forth. If this be the question of importance in practical affairs, by so much the more is it of importance in the affairs of faith, which determine the duties of mankind. The same may be said of the doctrine of moral duties. The misfortunes and misery of mankind arise less from an ignorance of duty than from a misconception of it—a recognition as duty of that which is not duty, and a rejection of that duty which is the chief. Bondareff asserts that the misfortune and misery of mankind arose from their accepting many empty and harmful regulations as religious duties, forgetting at the same time, and concealing from themselves and others, the first, chief and indubitable obligation enounced in the first chapters of the Holy Scriptures : 'In the sweat of thy face shalt thou eat bread.'

Bondareff says in one place that, were people once to accept 'bread-labour' as a religious duty, no particular private occupation could hinder them from performing it, just as no special occupation can induce Churchmen to work on their feast-days. There are in Russia more than eighty feast-days in the year, whereas to accomplish one man's share of 'bread-labour' only forty days are required. However strange it may seem at first that so simple a means, one that may be understood by all, and containing nothing difficult or involved, should be sufficient to cure all the innumerable existing ills of humanity, it is stranger still, as will appear when the question is investigated, that we, with such a simple, patent means, and one which has long been recognised, at our hands, should, leaving it on one side, seek to cure our ills by various intricate and difficult combinations. Only think over the subject, and you will see that it is so.

The teaching of Bondareff brings us back to this first indubitable duty in the sphere of practical activity. He proves that the performance of this duty hinders nothing, presents no obstacles, and withal saves men from the calamities of want and vice. The performance of this duty, to begin with, puts an end to that dreadful division of mankind into two classes which hate each other, and by mutual advances will cover that hatred. 'Bread-labour,' says Bondareff, will level all men, and will clip the wings of sensuality and luxury. It is impossible to plough or to dig wells in fine clothes, and with clean hands, and whilst feeding upon delicate dishes. Their occupation in one sacred work common to all will bring men into union. 'Bread-labour' will give intelligence to those who have lost it by a withdrawal from the natural line of mankind, and will bring happiness and content to people who have an undoubtedly useful and joyous occupation assigned to them by God Himself or by the laws of nature. 'Bread-labour' is the remedy which will save the human race.

I am afraid of injuring you, whoever you are who may read me, by the pride of my mind and by my own coldness. And I only ask you not to argue, not to prove, but question your heart alone. Whoever you may be, however richly gifted, however kind to those around you, in whatever circumstances you may be, can you be easy at your lunch, your dinner, in your affairs of State, your artistic, scientific, medical, pedagogic employments, while you can hear or see upon your doorstep a hungry, cold, sick, weary man? No? But they are always there, or if not upon your doorstep, ten yards or ten miles away—there they are, and you know it. . . . Go to the bottom, or what seems to you to be the bottom—it is really the top; place yourself beside those that feed the hungry and clothe the naked; fear nothing; worse it cannot be with you than it was, but it will be better every way. Stand in line with them; begin with your weak, unpractised hands the first work that feeds the hungry and clothes the naked: begin the 'bread-labour,' the struggle with nature, and for the first time you will feel solid ground under your feet; you will feel to be at home, free and steadfast, and that you need go no farther. You will experience those real unpoisoned joys which can be found nowhere else; no, not behind doors and curtains. You shall know joys unknown before, and for the first time become acquainted with those strong, simple men, your brothers, who, far from you, have fed you until now; and to your astonishment you shall find in them virtues you have not known, and modesty and kindness to you in especial, which you shall feel you have not deserved. Where you looked for irony and contempt you shall meet with caresses and gratitude and respect, because, having lived upon them and despised them all your life, you have suddenly bethought yourself and tried to help them with unaccustomed hands.—*The Triumph of Labour.*

There are three means of alleviating the condition of the labourers and of setting up brotherhood among men. 1. Not to make people work for you; neither directly nor indirectly to demand work of them; not to need such articles as demand extra labour—all objects of luxury. 2. To do for oneself, and, *if possible*, for others also that work which is tedious and unpleasant. 3. Not in reality a means, but the result and application of the second, to study the laws of nature and invent processes for the alleviation of labour—machinery, steam, electricity. One will invent what is really needed, and nothing superfluous, *only* when one invents in order to lighten one's own labour, or at least labour which one has oneself experienced.—*Some Social Remedies.*

No! dear friend, you are not right—not in what you say, but in *how* you say it. Do what you like, how you like; yet one thing only is necessary to God, to man, and to myself—it is that I should have a heart free from condemnation, contempt, irritation, irony, animosity towards men. And the devil take all this manual labour if it removes my heart from men, and does not draw me closer to them; it would be better, like a Buddhist, to go about with a bowl, begging.

The idolatry of labour is a dangerous error and a most habitual one. Prayer, as the result of one's aspiration towards God, is a most lawful act; but when it becomes an aim in itself, it produces ritual, which kills the moral life. Mercy, help afforded one's neighbour as the result of love to God, is a most lawful thing; but when it becomes an aim in itself, it produces philanthropy. Want, poverty, absence of property, as the result of abstinence from violent resistance and of renunciation of independent means, is a most lawful state; but when it is placed as a necessary condition, as an aim in itself, it produces the formal poverty of Buddhists and of monks. It is the same with manual labour. Such labour as the result of the renunciation of independent means and of the desire to serve others is a lawful thing, but if it becomes an aim in itself, it will inevitably lead to evil. But, above all—above all, I say to you from soul to soul, dear friend, the chief aim, infinite, joyful, always attainable, and worthy of the powers which are given us, is the increase of love. And increase of love is attainable by one definite effort—by the cleansing of one's soul from all that is personal, lustful, inimical.—*Letters on the Personal Christian Life.*

I was always astonished at the accepted opinion (current especially in Europe) that work is a kind of virtue. I always felt that it was only excusable in an irrational animal, such as the ant in the fable, to elevate work to the rank of a virtue and to make a boast of it. Even if work is not a vice it can from no point of view be looked upon as a merit. Work can no more be considered a virtue than can nutrition; work is a necessity of which one cannot be deprived without suffering, and to elevate it to the rank of a merit is as monstrous as it would be to do the like for nutrition. Work, the exercise of our organs, cannot be meritorious, for it is simply a physical necessity of man in common with all other animals, as is shown by a tethered calf galloping round and round, or, among ourselves, by the silly exercises to which rich and well-fed people of the leisure classes betake themselves, finding no better use for their mental faculties than reading novels and newspapers or playing chess and cards, nor for their muscles than gymnastics, fencing, lawn-tennis and horse-racing. In my opinion not only is work not a virtue, but in our defectively organised society it is more often a means of moral anæsthesia, just as are tobacco, wine, and other means of drowning thought and hiding from ourselves the disorder and emptiness of our lives.—*Stop and Think!*

IV.—THE LAW OF PURITY

The ideal is perfect chastity, in thought no less than in deed; and the commandment which enjoins purity—in married life forbidding adultery—is one which every man who is striving to attain this ideal must not do less than obey.—*The Kingdom of God is Within You.*

'It was easy to catch me' (said Pozdnischeff), 'seeing that I had been brought up under conditions calculated to breed young lovers, somewhat as cucumbers are forced in hot-houses. . . . Ecstasies, tenderness, and poetry were all there, in appearance at least, but in reality my love was the result of the contrivances of the mamma and the dressmaker on the one hand, and good dinners and inactivity on the other. If matchmaking by professional matchmakers is found to be debasing, our system is a thousand times more degrading, for, in the former case, the rights and chances are equal on both sides, whereas in the latter the woman is either a slave in the market or a mere decoy. It is strange that while, on the one hand, women are reduced to the lowest degree of humiliation, they are all-powerful on the other. Their position in that respect is perfectly analagous to that of the Jews. . . . Millions of people, generations of slaves, perish in the penal servitude of the factories merely in order to satisfy the whim of woman. Women, like empresses, condemn to imprisonment and hard labour nine-tenths of mankind. Such is the form assumed by their vengeance on us men for having degraded them and deprived them of equal rights. . . . Why is it, let me ask you, that games of hazard are prohibited, while women attired in meretricious costumes are not prohibited? And yet the latter are a thousand times more dangerous than the former!'

'Woman's serfdom consists in the circumstance that she is looked upon and sought after as an instrument of pleasure, and that this view is considered the right one. And then woman is solemnly enfranchised, is invested with extensive rights, equal to those exercised by men, but people continue to regard her as an instrument of pleasure, continue to educate her accordingly, instilling those views into her mind first in her childhood, and later on by means of public opinion. And so she remains what she was—a degraded, demoralised serf, as the man remains what he was—a demoralised slave-owner.'

'Why should the human race be perpetuated?' he

asked. 'Why?' I exclaimed, 'because otherwise we should not exist.' 'But why should we exist? If there be no purpose, no aim, if life be given to us for life's sake only, then there is no object in living. And if that be so, Schopenhauer and the Buddhists are perfectly right. On the other hand, if there be an end and object in human existence, it is clear that humanity must cease to exist when that object is attained. This is perfectly evident,' he repeated with visible emotion. 'If we succeed in rooting up the passions, and with them this last and most powerful, the prophecies will come to pass; men will be united by the bond of love, the aim and mission of humanity will have been fulfilled, and there will be no longer any reason for the further existence of the human race.'—*The Kreutzer Sonata.*

Within my memory has begun the deviation from the law by woman, that is to say, her fall; and within my memory it has proceeded farther and farther. A woman who has lost the law believes that her power consists in the charms of her witchery or in her skill at a pharisaic pretence of intellectual labour. But children hinder the one and the other. Therefore, with the help of science, within my memory it has come to pass that among the wealthy classes scores of means of destroying progeny have appeared. The evil has spread far and spreads farther every day. It will soon grasp all the women of the wealthy classes, and then they will become even with men, and together with them will lose every reasonable sense of life.

But there is yet time. If only women would understand their worth, their power, and would use them for the work of salvation of their husbands, brothers, and children, of all men. . . . You women and mothers who submit consciously to the law of God, you are the only ones who in our miserable, mutilated world, which has lost all semblance of humanity, know the true meaning of life and can show men true happiness. You are the only ones who know the joy and happiness which is the share of those who do not deviate from God's law. You know the joy of love to your husband—a joy never ending, never destroyed, like all other joys, but forming the beginning of another new joy—love to your child. You are the only ones who know, not the farcical pretence of labour, but that true labour which is imposed by God upon men, and know the rewards for it. You know it when, after the joys of love, you expect with emotion, fear, and hope, the torturing state of pregnancy, after which comes the bliss known to you only. You know it when, directly after those sufferings, without rest, without interruption, you undertake another series of labours and sufferings—those of nursing; for the sake of which you subjugate to your feeling, and renounce, the strongest human necessity, that of sleep, which, according to the saying, is sweeter than father and mother. And for months and years you do not sleep two nights running, and often you do not sleep whole nights; walking alone to and fro, rocking in your wearied arms an ailing baby, whose sufferings tear your heart. And when you do all this, unapproved and unseen by anybody, not expecting any praise or reward for it; when you do this, not as a great deed, but as the labourer of the gospel parable who came from the field, considering that you are only doing your duty, you know then what is false, fictitious labour—for human fame—and what is true labour—the fulfilment of God's will, the indication of which you feel in your heart.

THE LAW OF PURITY

When you are like this—and there are yet such women, happily for men—the same law you will apply also to the life of your husband, your children, and of men near you. You will encourage your husband to do the same labour, you will value and appreciate the worth of men by it, and for it you will prepare your children. . . . Such a woman will not only discourage her husband from false, sham labour, the only aim of which is to profit by other people's work, but will view with disgust and dread an activity that will serve as a double temptation for her children. Such a woman will not choose her daughter's husband according to the whiteness of his hands and the refinement of his manners, but, knowing thoroughly what is labour and what deceit, will always and everywhere, beginning with her husband, respect and appreciate men, will claim from them true labour with waste and danger of life, and will scorn that false, sham labour which has for its aim the delivering of one's self from true labour. Such a mother will bring forth and nurse her children herself, and, above all things else, will feed and provide for them, will work for them, wash and teach them, will sleep and talk with them, because she makes that her life-work. Only such a mother will not seek for her children external security through her husband's money, or her children's diplomas, but she will exercise in them the same capacity of self-sacrificing fulfilment of God's will which she knows in herself, the capacity for bearing labour with waste and danger of life, because she knows that only in that lie the security and welfare of life. Such a mother will not have to ask others what is her duty; she will know everything beforehand, and will fear nothing.

Only a mother before her death can say to Him who

sent her into this world, and to Him whom she has served by bearing and bringing up children, beloved by her more than herself—only she can peacefully say, after having served Him in her appointed service,—

'" Now lettest thou thy servant depart in peace."'

And this is that highest perfection to which, as to the highest good, men aspire. Such women who fulfil their mission, are those who reign over reigning men, those who prepare new generations of men and form public opinion; and therefore in the hands of these women lies the highest power of men's salvation from the existing and threatening evils of our time. Yes, women, mothers, in your hands, more than in those of any others, lies the salvation of the world!—*What then is to be Done?*

If we could look into the hearts of the majority of people, what should we find they most desire? Appetite for breakfast and for dinner. What is the severest punishment from infancy upwards? To be put on bread and water. What artisans get the highest wages? Cooks. What is the chief interest of the mistress of the house? To what subject does the conversation of middle-class housewives generally tend? It all comes round to the subject of eating, the price of grouse, the best way of making coffee, of baking sweet cakes, etc. In the middle and lower classes it is perfectly evident that every festivity, every funeral or wedding, means gluttony.

Many English men and women, for some reason or other, are specially proud of using a great deal of soap and pouring a large quantity of water over themselves.

There never has been, and cannot be, a good life

without abstinence. Apart from abstinence no good life is imaginable. The attainment of goodness must begin with it. ... Abstinence is the liberation of man from desires—their subordination to reasonableness—σωφροσύνη. But a man's desires are many and various, and in order successfully to contend with them he must begin with the fundamental ones—those upon which the more complicated ones have grown up—and not with those complex lusts which have grown up upon the fundamental ones. ... A man who eats too much cannot strive against laziness; while a gluttonous and idle man will never be able to contend with sexual lust. Therefore, according to all the moral teachings, the effort towards abstinence commences with a struggle against the lust of gluttony—commences with fasting. ... Fasting is an indispensable condition of a good life, whereas gluttony is, and always has been, the first sign of the opposite—a bad life; and unfortunately this vice is in the highest degree characteristic of the life of the majority of the men of our time.

Fasting! And even an analysis of how to fast, and where to begin! The notion seems ridiculous to the majority of men. I remember how an evangelical preacher, who was attacking monastic asceticism and priding himself on his originality, once said to me, 'My Christianity is not concerned with fasting and privations, but with beefsteaks.' Christianity, or virtue in general—with beefsteaks!

What, then, do I wish to say? That in order to be moral people must cease to eat meat? Not at all. I only wish to say that for a good life a certain order of good actions is indispensable; that if a man's aspiration toward right living be serious, it will inevitably follow one definite sequence, and that in this sequence the first virtue a man will strive after will be abstinence, self-renunciation. And in seeking to be abstinent a man will inevitably follow one definite sequence, and in this sequence the first thing will be abstinence in food, fasting. And in fasting, if he be really and seriously seeking to live a good life, the first thing from which he will abstain will always be the use of animal food, because, to say nothing of the excitation of the passions caused by such food, its use is simply immoral, as it involves the performance of an act which is contrary to the moral feeling—killing; and is called forth only by greediness and the desire for tasty food.— *The First Step.*

V.—THE LAW OF SACRIFICE

If people of the affluent class—say a man and woman —have left town life and have settled in the village in order to attempt to realise the brotherhood of man, this attempt must, if they are sincere, inevitably bring them into a terrible position. With their habits (formed from childhood upwards) of order, comfort, and especially of cleanliness, they, on moving to the village, after buying or hiring a hut, have cleared it of insects, perhaps even papered it themselves, and installed some remains, not luxurious but necessary, of their furniture—say an iron bedstead, a cupboard, and a writing-table. And so they begin life. At first the country folk shun them; expect them (like other rich people) to defend their advantages by force, and therefore do not approach them with requests and demands. But presently, bit by bit, the

THE LAW OF SACRIFICE

disposition of the newcomers gets known; they themselves offer gratuitous services, and the boldest and most insistent of the villagers find out practically that these newcomers do not refuse to give, and that one can get something out of them. Thereupon, all kinds of demands begin to be made upon them and constantly increase. . . . Not only do they feel the need of giving away their superfluity till they have only as much left as each one (say as the average man) ought to have, but, there being no possible definition of this 'average'—no way of measuring the amount which each one should have—there is no possibility of stopping, for crying want is always around them, and they have a surplus compared with this destitution. . . . They would have kept tea and food, but had to give it to some old pilgrims who were exhausted. At least it seemed right to keep the house clean, but beggar boys come and are allowed to spend the night, and again lice breed, after one has just got rid of those picked up during a visit to a sick man. Where and how can one stop? . . . The fact is, no such point of stoppage can exist; and if such a limit be found, it only proves that the feeling which prompted these people's act was imaginary or feigned.

What is one to do? Not to draw back means to lose one's life, to be eaten by lice, to starve, to die, and—apparently—uselessly. To stop is to repudiate that for the sake of which one has acted, for which one has done whatever good has been accomplished. And one cannot repudiate it, for it is no invention of mine, or of Christ's, that we are brothers and must serve each other; it is real fact, and when it has once entered you can never tear that consciousness out of the heart of man . . . Therefore, in our society the struggle against force

does not, for him who would live in brotherhood, eliminate the necessity of yielding up his life, of being eaten by lice, and of dying, whilst at the same time always striving against violence, preaching non-resistance, exposing violence, and above all giving an example of non-resistance and of self-sacrifice. Dreadful and difficult as is the position of a man living the Christian life, amidst the life of violence, he has no path but that of struggle and sacrifice—sacrifice without end. One must realise the gulf that separates the verminous, famished millions from the over-fed, over-dressed rich; and to fill up this gulf we need sacrifices, and not the hypocrisy with which we now try to hide from ourselves the depth of the gulf. A man may lack the strength to throw himself into the gulf—but it cannot be escaped by anyone who seeks after life. We may be unwilling to go into it, but let us be honest about it, and say so, and not deceive ourselves with hypocritical pretences. And, after all, the gulf is not so terrible. Or, if it be terrible, yet the horrors which await us in a worldly way of life are more terrible still. . . . Only that love is true love which knows no limit of sacrifice—even unto death.
—*The Root of the Evil.*

Mingle with a crowd, especially a town crowd; look at those harassed, agitated, sickly faces; recall your own life and that of those you have known intimately; remember the violent deaths, the cases of suicide of which you have heard—and then ask yourself the cause of all those miseries, and of that despair which ends in self-murder. You will see, terrible as it seems, that nine-tenths of human sufferings spring from the teaching of the world; that all these sufferings are really needless, and yet unavoidable, and that the majority of men are

THE LAW OF SACRIFICE

martyrs to the teaching of the world. . . . The teaching of the world says—Leave house, and fields, and brothers, leave the village for the unhealthy town, pass your life in a hot bathroom lathering strangers, or as a petty tradesman counting coppers in a shop like a cellar; or as a public prosecutor in trials, immersed in papers, and occupied in making the lives of unhappy wretches still worse; or as a State minister, always signing in haste useless documents; or as a captain, always bent on killing others—live this unnatural life, that must end in a painful death, and you shall receive nothing either in this world or in the world to come! And this call all obey.

Christ says—Take up thy cross and follow me; that is, bear patiently the lot awarded thee, and obey God; yet none obey. But the first worthless man, fitted for nothing but murder, who wears epaulettes, and takes it into his head to say, Take not up a cross, but a knapsack and gun, and follow me to inflict and undergo misery and certain death, is listened to and obeyed by all. Abandoning family, parents, wives and children, dressed like buffoons, and obeying the will of the first man of higher rank they meet, starving, worn out by long marches, they follow they know not where, like a herd of cattle to a slaughter-house. But they are not cattle, they are men. They cannot but know whither they are driven. With the unanswered question of 'Why?' on their lips, with despair in their hearts, they march to die from cold, and hunger, and disease, from the fire of bullets and cannon balls. They slay and are slain; yet not one of them knows why or wherefore this is so. They are roasted alive, flayed, disembowelled; but the next day, at the call of the trumpet, the survivors march with their eyes open to suffering and death. Yet no one finds any difficulty in obeying such commands. Not only the sufferers themselves, but their fathers and mothers see no difficulty; nay, they even urge their children to disobedience.

There were, it is said, at one time Christian martyrs, but they were exceptions; it has been calculated that their number has reached 380,000 during eighteen hundred years. But if we count the martyrs to the world, for every single martyr to Christ we shall find a thousand martyrs to the world, whose sufferings have been a hundred-fold greater. By death in wars alone during the nineteenth century have fallen thirty millions of men! These men were all martyrs to the teaching of the world. Putting the teachings of Christ aside, had they but forborne to follow that of the world what sufferings and death would they have escaped!

Christ calls us to no sacrifice; on the contrary, he offers us not the worse but the better part of life. Loving all men, he teaches them to refrain from maintaining themselves by violence, and from the mere heaping up of riches, even as men teach men to refrain from brawls and drunkenness. He tells men that, living without violence and without property, they will be happier than they are now, and by the example of his life confirms his words. He tells them that, living after his teaching, they must be prepared to die at any moment by violence or cold or hunger, and must not calculate on a single hour of life. And this seems to us a terrible demand for victims. Yet it is only a confirmation of the conditions under which every one of us inevitably lives. The disciple of Christ should be prepared at every instant for suffering and death. But is not the disciple of the world exactly in the same position? . . . Truly, all that we do to secure to ourselves prosperity is exactly what the ostrich does, who hides his head that he may not see his death. Nay, we do worse than the ostrich; for in order doubtfully to assure our lives in a doubtful future, we certainly spoil them in what might be a certain present. . . . Devoting our whole life to making preparations for its security, we have no time at all for life itself.—*My Religion.*

CHAPTER IV

SCIENCE, FALSE AND TRUE

WORK for science? But the word science is a term so vague and ill-defined that what some people consider to be science is considered by others to be utterly futile, and this is the case not only with outsiders but even with the priests of science themselves. While those savants who favour a spiritual explanation of life look upon jurisprudence, philosophy, and even theology as the most necessary and important of sciences, the Positivists consider these very sciences as childish twaddle devoid of scientific value; and *vice versâ*, sociology, which the Positivists look upon as the science of sciences, is considered by the theologians, philosophers, and spiritualists as an arbitrary and useless collection of observations and assertions. But more than this, even in one and the same branch of philosophy or natural science each system has ardent defenders and equally ardent detractors, equally competent, yet holding diametrically opposite opinions. Finally, does not each year witness fresh scientific discoveries, which, after exciting the wonder of the mediocrities of the whole world, and bringing fame and fortune to their inventors, are eventually found to be nothing but ridiculous errors even by those who promulgated them?

Just as it was not exactly in the creation of the world in six days, the wound-curing serpent, etc., that the

Hebrew believed, but rather in the infallibility of his priests, and hence in the truth of their assertions, even so the great majority of the cultured people of our time believe neither in the formation of the world by rotation, nor in heredity, nor in comma-bacilli, but in the infallibility of their lay priests who are called scientists, who affirm whatever they pretend to know with the same assurance as did the Hebrew priests. I will even say that if the priests of old, amenable to no control save that of their colleagues, permitted themselves sometimes to digress from the truth merely for the pleasure of astonishing and mystifying their public, the priests of modern science have done as much with equal effrontery. The greater part of what is called religion is but the superstition of the past; the greater part of what is called science is no more than the superstition of the present day. The proportion of error and of truth is, I suspect, about the same in the one as in the other.—*Stop and Think!*

Science, by isolating the agents of production, declares that the natural condition of a working man—that is, of a man in the true sense of the word—is that unnatural condition in which he exists at present, as in ancient times, by the division of men into citizens and slaves. The question of economical science is this: What is the reason of the fact that some men by means of money acquire an imaginary right to the land and capital, and may make slaves of those men who have no money? The answer which presents itself to common sense would be, that it is the result of money, the nature of which is to enslave men. But science denies this, and says, This arises, not from the nature of money, but from the fact that some men have land

and capital, and others have neither. We ask why persons who possess land and capital oppress such as possess neither? and we are answered, Because they do possess land and capital. But this is just what we are inquiring about. Is not deprivation of land and tools enforced slavery? Life ceases not to put this essential question: and even science herself notices it, and tries to answer it, but does not succeed in doing so; proceeding from her own fundamental principles, she only turns herself round, as in a magic circle.

If the object of this sham, so-called science of Political Economy had not been the same as that of all other sciences of law—the justification of violence—it could not have avoided noticing the strange phenomenon that the distribution of wealth, and the depriving of some men of land and capital, and the enslaving of some men by others, depend upon money, and that it is only by means of money that some men utilise the labour of others; in other words, enslave them. But science, with full assurance, asserts that money has no connection whatever with the matter in question. . . . Wherever there is in society the mastery of one man over another, there the meaning of money as the measure of value at once yields to the will of the oppressor, and its meaning as a medium of exchange of the productions of labour is replaced by another, that of the most convenient means of utilising the labour of others.

The position of men living by other men's labour is based not only upon a certain belief but upon an entire doctrine, and not only on one doctrine but on three which have grown one upon another and are now fused into an awful deceit, or humbug, as the English call it, which hides from men their unrighteousness. The oldest of these in our world, which justifies the treason of men against the fundamental duty of labour for a livelihood, was the Church-Christian doctrine, according to which men, by the will of God, differ one from another, some men being ordained to have dominion over others, and the remainder being ordained to obey. This doctrine, though already shaken to its foundations, still continues to influence some men, so that many who do not accept it, who often even ignore the existence of it, are, nevertheless, guided by it. The second is what I cannot help terming the State-Philosophical doctrine. According to it, as fully developed by Hegel, all that exists is reasonable, and the established order of life is constant and sustained, not merely by men, but as the only possible form of the manifestation of the spirit, or, generally, of the life of mankind. . . . The last doctrine, on which is based the justification as well of leading statesmen as of leading men of business and of science and art, is a scientific one, not in the evident sense of the word, meaning knowledge generally, but in the sense of a knowledge peculiar in form as well as in matter, termed science in particular. This new doctrine appeared in Europe contemporaneously with a large class of rich and idle people, who served neither the Church nor the State, and who were in want of a justification of their position. . . . But as time went on, this class of rich people, who did not belong either to the clergy, to the government, or to the army, owing to the vices of these three classes, increased in number, and became a powerful party. They were in want of a justification of their position. And one was invented for them. . . . And what is still more wonderful is this, that the former servants of Church, State, and army, do not now lean upon the divineness of their calling, nor even upon the philosophy which considers the State necessary for individual development; but they set aside these supports which have so long maintained them, and are now seeking the same supports on which the new reigning class of men, who have found a novel justification, stands, and at the head of which are the men of science and art. . . . According to the scientific doctrine it is only sociology based upon biology, based again upon all other positive sciences, which is able to give us new laws of the life of mankind. If some men govern, and others obey, some live in opulence, and others in want, then this takes place, neither according to the will of God, nor because the State is the form of the manifestation of personality, but because in societies as in organisms a division of labour takes place which is necessary for the life of the whole. Some men perform in societies the muscular part of labour and others the mental. Upon this doctrine is built the ruling excuse of the age.

Modern science selects its facts upon the ground of a determinate theory, which sometimes it knows, sometimes does not wish to know, sometimes really does not know; but it exists. And the theory is this: All mankind is an undying organism; men are particles of the organs of this organism, having each his special calling for the service of the whole. As the cells, growing into an organism, divide among themselves the labour of the struggle for existence of the whole organism, increase one capacity, and diminish another, and all together form an organ in order better to satisfy the wants of the whole organism; and as among social animals—ants and bees—the individuals divide the labour among themselves, so also in mankind and in human societies there takes place the same differentiation and integration of the parts. . . . These facts lead to one thing—the acknowledgment that the existence in human societies of division of activities is organic, that is, necessary. And they therefore induce us to consider the unjust position in which we are, who have freed ourselves from labouring, not from the point of reasonableness and justice, but merely as an indubitable fact which confirms a general law. Moral philosophy used also to justify every cruelty and wickedness; but there it turned out to be philosophical, and therefore incorrect; but according to science, the same thing turns out to be scientific, and therefore unquestionable. . . . And it is upon this new belief that the justification of idleness and the cruelty of men is built.

All this edifice was built upon the sand, upon an arbitrary and incorrect assertion that mankind, collectively considered, was an organism. This assertion was incorrect, because mankind lacks the essential characteristic of an organism—a centre of sensation or consciousness; and therefore, however many other general character-signs we may find out in mankind and in an organism, without this the acknowledgment of mankind to be an organism is incorrect. But notwithstanding the arbitrariness and incorrectness of the fundamental proposition of positive philosophy, it was accepted by the so-called educated world with great sympathy, because of that great fact, important for the crowd, that it afforded a justification of the existing order of things by recognising the lawfulness of the existing division of labour, that is, of violence in mankind. . . . And now there appeared a similarly arbitrary and incorrect assertion, not a new one at all, to the effect that all living beings proceed one from another, not only one organism from another but one from many, an assertion that has not been and cannot be verified, and must remain a mere supposition. . . . According to the theory of evolution, it appears that the variety of species of living beings proceeded by themselves in consequence of the infinite variety of conditions of inheritance and environment in an infinite period of time. The theory of evolution, speaking plainly, asserts only that by chance in an infinite period of time anything you like may proceed from anything else you choose. This is no answer to the question; it is simply the same question put differently: instead of will is put chance, and the co-efficient of the infinite is transferred from omnipotence to time. But this new assertion, enforced by Darwin's followers in an arbitrary and inaccurate spirit, maintained the former assertion of Comte, and therefore it became a revelation for our time, and the foundation of all sciences, even that of the history of philosophy and religion; and besides, according to the *naïve* confession of the very founder of Darwin's theory, this idea was awakened in him by the law of Malthus; and therefore he pointed to the struggle for existence not only of men, but of all living beings, as to a fundamental law of every living thing. And this was exactly what was wanted by the crowd of idle people for their own justification. Two unstable theories which could not stand upon their own feet supported each other, and received a show of stability.

The new deceit, the scientific one, is exactly such as the old ones were; its essence consists in the substitution for reason and conscience of something external; and this external thing is observation, as, in theology it was revelation. The snare of this science consists in this: that, having shown men the most barefaced perversions of the activity of reason and conscience, it destroys in them confidence in both reason and conscience. These men lose the conception of good and evil; all is, in their slang, conditional and subjective.... The credulous crowd of youth, overwhelmed by the novelty of this authority, not only not destroyed but not yet even touched by criticism, rush to the study of these facts of natural sciences as to the only way which can lead to the elucidation of all questions of life. But the farther they proceed in this study, the farther do they remove not only the possibility of solving the questions of life, but even the very thought of this solution; the more they grow accustomed not so much to observe themselves as to believe upon their word other men's observations (to believe in cells, in protoplasm, in the fourth dimension of matter, and so on); the more the form hides from them the contents: the more they lose the consciousness of good and evil; but chiefly they pass their best years in losing the habit of life, that is, of labouring, and accustom themselves to consider their own position justified, and thus become physically good-for-nothing parasites, and mentally dislocate their brains, and lose all power of thought-productiveness. And so, by degrees, their capacities more and more blunted, they acquire self-assurance, which deprives them for ever of the possibility of returning to a simple, laborious life, to any plain, clear, common, human manner of thinking.

We are the brain of the people. They feed us, and we have undertaken to teach them. Only for the sake of this have we freed ourselves from labour. What, then, have we been teaching them? They have waited years, tens of years, hundreds of years. And we are still conversing among ourselves, and teaching each other, and amusing ourselves, and have quite forgotten them. We have so totally forgotten them that others have taken upon themselves to teach and amuse them, and we have not even become aware of this in our flippant talk about division of labour; and it is very obvious that all our talk about the utility we offer to the people was only a shameful excuse.

Science and art have done much for mankind, not because, but in spite of, the fact that men of science and art, under the pretext of division of labour, live upon the shoulders of the working people. . . . We are so accustomed to our pampered or debilitated representatives of intellectual labour that it would seem very strange if a learned man or an artist were to plough or cart manure. We think that, were he to do so, all would go to ruin, that all his wisdom would be shaken out of him, and the great artistic images he carries in his breast would be soiled by the manure; but we are so accustomed to our present conditions that we do not wonder at our ministers of science, that is, ministers and teachers of truth, compelling other people to do for them that which they could very well do themselves, passing half their time eating, smoking, chattering in 'liberal' gossip, reading newspapers, novels, visiting theatres. We are not surprised to see our philosopher in an inn, in a theatre, at a ball; we do not wonder when we learn that those artists who delight and ennoble our souls pass their lives in drunkenness, in playing cards, in company with loose women, or do things still worse.

'But science! art! You repudiate science, art; that

is, you repudiate that by which mankind live.' I am always hearing this. But it is unjust. I not only do not repudiate science—human reasonable activity,—and art—the expression of this reasonable activity,—but it is only in the name of this reasonable activity and its expression that I say what I do, in order that mankind may avoid the savage state towards which they are rapidly moving, owing to the false teaching of our time. Science and art are as necessary to men as food, drink, and clothes—even still more necessary than these; but they become such, not because we decide that what we call science and art are necessary, but because they indeed are necessary to men. . . . Since men have existed, they have always had science in the plainest and largest sense of the word. Science, as the sum of all human information, has always been in existence; and without it life is not conceivable, and there is no necessity whatever either to attack or to defend it.

But the region of this knowledge is so various, so much information of all kinds enters into it, that man would be lost if he had no clue which could help him to decide which of all these kinds of information is more, and which less, important. . . . Since mankind has existed, in every nation, teachers have appeared to form science in this strict sense—the science about what it is most necessary for men to know. This science has always had for its object the inquiry as to what was the destiny, and therefore the true welfare, of each man and of all men. This science has served as a clue in determining the importance and the expression of all other sciences. Such was the science of Confucius, Buddha, Moses, Socrates, Christ, Mohammed—science as it has been understood by all men except by our own circle of so-called educated people. Such a science has not only always occupied the first place, but it is the one science which has determined the importance of other sciences. . . . Without knowledge as to what constitutes the calling and welfare of all men, all other arts and sciences become, as is really the case at present with us, only an idle and pernicious amusement.

The business of science is to serve people. We have invented telegraphs, telephones, phonographs, but what improvements have we made in the life of the people? We have catalogued two millions of insects; but have we domesticated a single animal since biblical times, when all our animals had long been domesticated, and still the elk and the deer and the partridge and the grouse and the wood-hen are wild? Botanists have discovered the cells, and in the cells protoplasms, and in protoplasms something else, and in this something else again. These occupations will evidently never end, and therefore learned men have no time to do anything useful. And hence from the times of the ancient Egyptians and Hebrews, when wheat and lentils were already cultivated, down to the present time, not a single plant has been added for the nourishment of the people except potatoes, and these have not been discovered by science. We have invented torpedoes, house-drains; but the spinning-wheel, weaving-looms, ploughs and axe-handles, flails and rakes, buckets and well-sweeps, are still the same as in the time of Rurik. And if some things have been improved, it is not the learned who have done it.

An engineer, a surgeon, a teacher, an artist, an author, seem by their very professions to be obliged to serve the people, but what do we see? With the present tendency, they can bring to the people nothing but harm. An engineer and a mechanic must work with capital: without capital they are good for nothing. ... The scientific co-operation for the people must be quite a different one. It will begin when a man of science, an engineer, or a surgeon, will cease to consider as lawful that division of labour, or rather that taking away other men's labour, which now exists, and when he no longer considers that he has the right to take, I do not say hundreds of thousands, but even a moderate sum of one thousand or five hundred roubles as a compensation for his services; but when such a man comes to live among labouring people in the same condition and in the same way as they, then he will apply his information in mechanics, technics, hygiene, to the curing of working people.

A true art and a true science have two unmistakable characteristics—the first, an interior one, that a minister of art or science fulfils his calling, not for the sake of gain, but with self-denial; and the second, an exterior one, that his productions are intelligible to all men, whose welfare he is aiming at.—*What then is to be Done?*

Edward Carpenter [in *Civilisation: Its Cause and Cure, and other Essays*] proves that neither astronomy, nor physics, nor chemistry, nor biology, nor sociology gives us a true knowledge of actual facts, but that all the 'laws' discovered by these sciences are only generalisations, which have but an approximate value as laws, and that only owing to ignorance or disregard of other factors. Further, that even these laws appear to be laws to us only because we discover them in a domain so distant from us in time and space that we cannot perceive their want of correspondence with actual fact. Besides this, Carpenter also points out that the method of science, consisting in the explanation of phenomena near and important to us by phenomena more distant from and indifferent to us, is a false method which can never lead to the desired results. . . . It is supposed that to reduce higher questions to terms of lower ones will explain the higher. But this explanation is never attained, and what happens is that, descending lower and lower in its investigations, from the most essential questions to those less essential, science at last reaches a domain quite foreign to man, and only adjacent to him, to which domain it confines its attention, leaving without any solution all questions most important for man.

Men must live. And in order to live they must know how to live. All men always—well or ill—have learnt this, and, in accordance with their knowledge, have lived and progressed. And this knowledge of how men should live was always, since the times of Moses, Solon, Confucius, considered a science — the very science of sciences; and it is only in our time that it has begun to be considered that the science of how to live is not a science at all, but that true science is only experimental science, beginning with mathematics and ending with sociology. And a strange misunderstanding ensues. A simple and sensible working man—according to the old sense and common sense as well—supposes that if there are men studying all their life, who think for him in return for being fed and provided for by him, then these men are probably engaged in studying what is needful for man; and he expects from science that it will solve for him those questions on which depend his welfare and that of all men. He expects that science will teach him how to live, how to act towards the members of his own family, his neighbours, and those of other countries; how to struggle with his passions; in what he should and should not believe, and much besides. And what does our science reply? It triumphantly announces how many millions of miles the sun is from the earth, how many millions of undulations of ether per second are produced by light, and how many undulations of atmosphere by sound; it tells of the chemical composition of the Milky Way; it tells of a new element, Helior, of micro-organisms and their excrements, of the points in the hand where electricity concentrates, of X rays, and so on.

True science has never been appreciated by its contemporaries, but, on the contrary, has for the most part been persecuted. And it could not be otherwise. True science indicates to men their errors, and points to new, unusual ways of life, both of which services are obnoxious to the ruling part of society; whereas the present science not only refrains from counteracting the tastes and demands of the ruling part of society, but completely coincides with them, satisfies idle curiosity, astonishes people, and promises them increase of pleasure. Whereas all that is truly great is quiet, modest, imperceptible, the science of our time knows no limits to its self-glorification. Yet, seen in its full significance, no science in any age or nation has stood on so low a plane as the present one. One part of it, that which should be a study of the means of making human life good and happy, is occupied in justifying the existing bad order of life, and the other is absorbed with the solution of questions of idle curiosity.—*Modern Science.*

CHAPTER V

ART, FALSE AND TRUE

ALMOST every educated man at the present day is striving unconsciously to preserve the old-time conception of society, which justifies his attitude, and to conceal from others and from himself its inconsistencies. Contemporary literature, philosophical, political and artistic, affords a striking proof of the truth of my statement. What wealth of imagination, what form and colour, what erudition and art, but what a lack of serious purpose, what reluctance to face any exact thought! Ambiguity of expression, indirect allusion, witticisms, vague reflection, but no straightforward or candid dealing with the subject they treat of, namely, life. Indeed, our writers treat of obscenities and improprieties; in the guise of refined paradox they convey suggestions which thrust men back to primeval savagery, to the lowest dregs not only of pagan life, but of animal life, which we outlived five thousand years ago.—*The Kingdom of God is Within You.*

That special gift called *genius* consists in the faculty of intense, strenuous attention, applied, according to the author's tastes, to this or that subject; and by means of which the possessor of this capacity sees the things to which he applies his attention in some new aspect overlooked by others. Three qualifications, in addition to genius, are indispensable to a true work of art. These are: (1) a correct, that is, a moral, relation of the author to his subject; (2) perspicuity or beauty of expression (the two are identical); and (3) sincerity, *i.e.*, an unfeigned feeling of love or hatred to the subject depicted.

The cement which binds together every work of art into a whole, and thereby produces the effect of life-like illusion, is not the unity of persons and places, but that of the author's independent moral relation to the subject. In reality, when we read or examine the art-work of a new author, the fundamental questions which arise in our mind are always of this kind: 'Well, what sort of a man are you? And what distinguishes you from all the people I know, and what information can you give me as to how we must look upon our life?' Whatever the artist depicts, whether it be saints or robbers, kings or lackeys, we seek and see only the soul of the artist himself. And if he be an established writer, with whom we are already acquainted, the question is no longer: 'Who are you?' but 'Well, what more can you tell me that is new? From what standpoint will you now illuminate life for me?' Therefore, a writer who has not a clear, definite, and fresh view of the universe, and especially a writer who does not even consider this necessary, cannot produce a work of art. He may write much and beautifully, but a work of art will not result.—*Guy de Maupassant and the Art of Fiction.*

To evoke in oneself a feeling one has once experienced, and having evoked it in oneself, then, by means of move-ments, lines, colours, sounds, or forms expressed in words, so to transmit that feeling that others may experience the same feeling—this is the activity of art. Art is a human activity consisting in this, that one man consciously, by means of certain external signs, hands on to others feelings he has lived through, and that other people are infected by these feelings, and also experience them. Art is not, as the metaphysicians say, the manifestation of some mysterious Idea of beauty, or God; it is not, as the æsthetical physiologists say, a game in which man lets off his excess of stored-up energy; it is not the expression of man's emotions by external signs; it is not the production of pleasing objects, and, above all, it is not pleasure; but it is a means of union among men, joining them together in the same feelings, and indispensable for the life and progress towards well-being of individuals and of humanity.

All human life is filled with works of art of every kind —from cradle-song, dance, jest, mimicry, up to church services, buildings, monuments, and triumphal processions. It is all artistic activity. Just as speech acts on us not only in sermons, orations and books, but in all that talk by which we transmit our thoughts and experiences to each other, so also art, in the wide meaning of the word, permeates our whole life, and it is only some of the manifestations of this art that we speak of as 'Art' in the narrow meaning of the word.

Humanity unceasingly moves forward from a lower, more partial and obscure understanding of life to one more general and more lucid. And in this, as in every movement, there are leaders. . . . Religions are the exponents of the highest comprehension of life accessible to the best and foremost men at a given time in a given society, a comprehension towards which, inevitably and irresistibly, all the rest of that society must advance. And therefore only religions have always served, and still serve, as bases for the valuation of human sentiments. . . . In every age, and in every human society, there exists a religious sense, common to that whole society, of what is good and what is bad, and it is this religious conception that decides the value of the feelings transmitted by art.

The highest perfection of goodness (not only not identical with beauty, but, for the most part, contrasting with it) which was discerned by the Jews even in the times of Isaiah, and fully expressed by Christianity, was quite unknown to the Greeks. They supposed that the beautiful must necessarily also be good. . . . Plato's reasonings about beauty and goodness are full of contradictions. And it was just this confusion of ideas that those Europeans of a later age who had lost all faith tried to elevate into a law. They tried to prove that this union of beauty and goodness is inherent in the very essence of things; that beauty and goodness must coincide; and that the word and conception καλο-κἀγαθόν (which had a meaning for Greeks, but has none at all for Christians) represents the highest ideal of humanity. On this misunderstanding the new science of æsthetics was built up. And to justify its existence, the teachings of the ancients on art were so twisted as to make it appear that this invented science of æsthetics had existed among the Greeks. In reality, the reasoning of the ancients on art was quite unlike ours.

If a theory justifies the false position in which a certain part of a society is living, then, however unfounded or even obviously false it may be, it is accepted, and becomes an article of faith to that section of society. Such, for instance, was the celebrated and unfounded theory expounded by Malthus of the tendency of the population of the world to increase in geometrical progression, but of the means of sustenance to increase only in arithmetical progression, and of the consequent over-population of the world; such, also, was the theory (an outgrowth of the Malthusian) of selection and struggle for existence as the basis of human progress. Such, again, is Marx's theory, which regards the gradual destruction of small private production by large capitalistic production now going on around us as an inevitable decree of fate. ... To this class belongs this astonishing theory of the Baumgartenian Trinity—Goodness, Beauty, and Truth. According to this theory, Goodness, Beauty, and Truth are different manifestations of the one essential perfection, and therefore are conceptions equal among themselves. What is important is that we have no ground for such an assertion. Goodness is really the fundamental metaphysical conception which forms the essence of our consciousness; it is a conception not defined by reason, it is that which can be defined by nothing else, but which defines everything else; it is the highest, the eternal aim of our life. ... The good is that which we call God. But beauty—if we do not want mere words, but speak about what we understand —beauty is nothing but what pleases us, and therefore the notion of beauty not only does not coincide with goodness, but rather is contrary to it, for the good most often coincides with victory over the passions, but beauty is at the root of all our passions. (I know that to this people always say that there is a moral and spiritual beauty, but this is merely playing with words, for by spiritual and moral beauty nothing else is understood but goodness.)

ART, FALSE AND TRUE

What we call truth is merely the correspondence of an expression, or of a definition of an object, with reality or with an understanding of the object common to everyone, and therefore it is a means of arriving at the good; but in itself truth is not goodness, and often it does not even coincide with it. With beauty truth has not even anything in common, but for the most part is in contradiction to it, for truth generally exposes the deception and destroys illusion, which is the chief condition of beauty.

Since the upper classes of the Christian nations lost faith in Church-Christianity, the art of those upper classes has separated itself from the art of the rest of the people, and there have been two arts—popular art and genteel art. . . . All the confused, unintelligible theories of art and its stagnation in its false path arise from the amazingly and palpably false assertion that the art of our upper classes is the whole of art, the true, the only, the universal art. . . . Even in our Christian society hardly one per cent. of the people make use of this art which we speak of as being the whole of art.

We hold that all people have equal rights, if not to material at any rate to spiritual well-being; and yet ninety-nine per cent. of our European population live and die, generation after generation, crushed by toil, much of which toil is necessary for the production of our art, which they never use; and we, nevertheless, calmly assert that the art which we produce is the real, true, only art—all of art! To the remark that, if our art is the true art, then everyone should have the benefit of it, the ordinary reply is that if not everybody at present makes use of existing art, the fault does not lie in the art, but in the false organisation of society; that one can imagine to oneself, in the future, a state of things in which physical labour will be partly superseded by machinery, partly lightened by its just distribution, and that labour for the production of art will be taken in turns; that there is no need for some people always to sit below the stage moving the decorations, winding up the machinery, and working at the piano or French horn, and setting type and printing books, but that the people who do all this work might be engaged only a few hours per day, and in their leisure time might enjoy all the blessings of art. That is what the defenders of our exclusive art say. But I think they do not themselves believe it. They cannot help knowing that fine art can arise only on the slavery of the masses of the people, and can continue only as long as that slavery lasts.

But even were we to admit the inadmissible, and say that means may be found by which art (that art which among us is considered to be art) may be obtainable by the whole people, another consideration presents itself, showing that fashionable art cannot be the whole of art, viz., the fact that it is completely unintelligible to the people. . . . Even if a possibility were given to the labouring classes, in their free time, to see, to read, and to hear all that forms the flower of contemporary art (as is done to some extent in towns, by means of picture galleries, popular concerts, and libraries), the working man (to the extent to which he is a labourer, and has not begun to pass into the ranks of those perverted by idleness) would be able to make nothing of our fine art, and if he did understand it, that which he understood would not elevate his soul, but would certainly, in most cases, pervert it. To thoughtful and sincere people there can therefore be no doubt that the art of our upper classes never can be the art of the whole people. But if art be an important matter, a spiritual blessing, essential for all men ('like religion,' as the devotees of art are fond of saying), then it should be accessible to everyone. And if, as in our day, a particular art is not accessible to all men, then one of two things: either art is not the vital matter that it is represented to be, or that art which we call art is not the real thing.

Apart from the moral effects such a perversion of art has had on European society, it has weakened art itself, and well-nigh destroyed it. The first great result was that art, by making enjoyment its aim, was deprived of the infinite, varied, and profound religious subject-matter proper to it. The second result was that, having only a small circle of people in view, it lost its beauty of form, and became affected and obscure; and the third and chief result was that it ceased to be either unconscious or sincere, and became thoroughly fictitious and artificial.

The assertion that art may be good art, and at the same time incomprehensible to a great number of people, is extremely unjust, and its consequences are ruinous to art itself. . . . And it turns out that those who say the majority do not understand good works of art still do not explain those works, but only tell us that, in order to understand them, one must read, and see, and hear these same works over and over again. But this is not to explain, but only to habituate! And people may habituate themselves to anything, even to the very worst things. As people may habituate themselves to bad food, to spirits, tobacco, and opium, just in the same way they may habituate themselves to bad art—and that is exactly what is being done.

Great works of art are only great because they are accessible and comprehensible to everyone. The story of Joseph, translated into the Chinese language, touches a Chinese. The story of Sakya Muni touches us. And there are, and must be, buildings, pictures, statues, and music of similar power. So that, if art fails to move men, it cannot be said that this is due to the spectators' or hearers' lack of understanding; but the conclusion to be drawn may, and should be, that such art is either bad art, or not art at all.

The business of art lies just in this—to make that understood and felt which, in the form of an argument, might be incomprehensible and inaccessible. Usually it seems to the recipient of a truly artistic impression that he knew the thing before, but had been unable to express it.

Universal art arises only when some one of the people, having experienced a strong emotion, feels the necessity of transmitting it to others. Professional, upper-class art, on the other hand, arises not from the artist's inner impulse, but chiefly because people of the upper classes demand amusement and pay well for it. . . . Artists therefore have had to devise methods of producing imitations of art in order to satisfy the demands of people of the upper classes. These methods are those of (1) borrowing, (2) ornamenting, (3) striking (effects), and (4) interesting.

An artistic impression, *i.e.*, infección, is only received

when an author has, in the manner peculiar to himself, experienced the feeling which he transmits, and not when he passes on another man's feeling previously transmitted to him. . . . All borrowing merely recalls to the reader, spectator, or listener, some dim recollection of artistic impressions they have received from previous works of art, and does not infect them with that feeling which the artist himself has experienced. A work founded on something borrowed, like Goethe's *Faust*, for instance, may be very well executed, and be full of mind and every beauty, but because it lacks the chief characteristic of a work of art—completeness, oneness, the inseparable unity of form and contents expressing the feeling the artist has experienced—it cannot produce a real artistic impression.

The sight of the most beautiful suffering may infect us very powerfully with a feeling of compassion, sympathy, or admiration for the self-sacrifice of the sufferer, while, on the other hand, the sight of an unquestionably beautiful wax figure may infect us with no feeling whatever. To estimate a work of art by the degree of beauty it possesses is, in fact, as strange as to judge of the fertility of soil by the beauty of its situation.

Neither does the method of imitating art by the use of what is striking or effective coincide with real art, for in effectfulness—the effects of novelty, of the unexpected, of contrasts, of the horrible—there is no transmission of feeling, but only an action on the nerves. If an artist were to paint a bloody wound admirably, the sight of the wound would strike me, but it would not be art. One prolonged note on a powerful organ will produce a striking impression, will often even cause tears, but there is no music in it, because no feeling is transmitted. Yet such physiological effects are constantly mistaken for art by people of our circle, and this not only in music, but also in poetry, painting and the drama. It is said that art has becomed refined. On the contrary, thanks to the pursuit of effectfulness, it has become very coarse.

To speak of an interesting work of art means either that we receive from a work of art information new to us, or that the work is not fully intelligible, and that, little by little, and with effort, we arrive at its meaning, and experience a certain pleasure in this process of guessing it. In neither case has the interest anything in common with artistic impression. Art aims at infecting people with feeling experienced by the artist. But the mental effort necessary to enable the spectator, listener, or reader to assimilate the new information contained in the work, or to guess the puzzles propounded, by distracting him, hinders the infection. And therefore it may be stated that the interestingness of a work not only has nothing to do with its excellence as a work of art, but rather hinders than assists artistic impression.

Many conditions must be fulfilled to enable a man to produce a real work of art. It is necessary that he should stand on the level of the highest life-conception of his time, that he should experience feeling, and have the desire and capacity to transmit it, and that he should, moreover, have a talent for some one of the forms of art. It is very seldom that all these conditions necessary to the production of true art are combined. Counterfeit art is diffused in our society in enormous quantities, and the number of such counterfeits is increasing more and more. Three conditions co-operate to cause this increase. They are—(1) the considerable remuneration of artists for their productions, (2) art criticism, and (3) schools of art.

As soon as the upper classes acclaimed every kind of art as good if only it afforded them pleasure, and began to reward such art more highly than any other social activity, immediately a large number of people devoted themselves to this activity, and art assumed quite a different character and became a profession. And as soon as this occurred, the chief and most precious quality of art—its sincerity—was at once greatly weakened and eventually quite destroyed, and art was replaced by counterfeits of art. The professional artist lives by his art, and has continually to invent subjects for his works, and does invent them. And it is obvious how great a difference must exist between works of art produced on the one hand by men such as the Jewish prophets, the authors of the Psalms, Francis of Assissi, the authors of the *Iliad* and *Odyssey*, of folk-stories, legends, and folk-songs, many of whom not only received no remuneration for their work, but did not even attach their names to it; and, on the other hand, works produced by Court poets, dramatists, and musicians receiving honours and remuneration, and later on by professional artists, who lived by the trade, receiving remuneration from newspaper editors, publishers, impressarios, and in general from those agents who come between the artists and the town public, the consumers of art. Professionalism is the first condition of the diffusion of false, counterfeit art.

The second condition is the growth, in recent times, of artistic criticism, *i.e.*, the valuation of art not by everybody, and, above all, not by plain men, but by erudite, that is, by perverted and at the same time self-confident individuals. Artistic criticism did not exist—could not and cannot exist—in societies where art is undivided, and where consequently it is appraised by the religious understanding-of-life common to the whole people. Art criticism grew, and could grow, only on the art of the upper classes, who did not acknowledge the religious perception of their time. Universal art has a definite and indubitable internal criterion—religious perception; upper-class art lacks this, and therefore the appreciators of that art are obliged to cling to some external criterion.

The chief harm done by the critics is this, that themselves lacking the capacity to be infected by art (and that is the characteristic of all critics; for did they not lack this they could not attempt the impossible—the interpretation of works of art), they pay most attention to, and eulogise, brain-spun, invented works; and set these up as models worthy of imitation. That is the reason they so confidently extol, in literature, the Greek tragedians, Dante, Tasso, Milton, Shakespeare, Goethe (almost all he wrote), and, among recent writers, Zola and Ibsen; in music, Beethoven's last period, and Wagner. . . . In this connection the instance of Beethoven is most striking. Among his innumerable productions there are, notwithstanding their artificiality of form, works of true art. But he grows deaf, cannot hear, and begins to write invented, unfinished works, which are consequently often meaningless and musically unintelligible. But criticism, having once acknowledged him to be a great composer, seizes on just these unfinished and often abnormal works with special gusto, and searches for extraordinary beauties in them. And (perverting the very meaning of musical art) to justify its laudations, it attributes to music the property of depicting what it cannot depict. And imitators appear—an innumerable host of imitators of these sickly, crippled works which Beethoven wrote when he was deaf, and which he never developed to the rank of art.

The third condition of the perversion of art, namely, art schools, is almost more harmful still. . . . Art is the transmission to others of a special feeling experienced by the artist. How can this be taught in schools? . . . No school can evoke feeling in a man, and still less can it teach him how to manifest it in the one particular manner natural to him alone. But the essence of art lies in these things. . . . The one thing these schools can teach is how to transmit feelings experienced by other artists in the way those other artists transmitted them; and such instruction . . . does more than anything else to deprive people of the capacity to understand true art. . . . Professional schools produce a hypocrisy of art precisely akin to that hypocrisy of religion which is produced by theological colleges for training priests, pastors, and religious teachers generally. As it is impossible in a school to train a man so as to make a religious teacher of him, so it is impossible to teach a man how to become an artist.

These three conditions—the professionalisation of artists, art criticism, and art schools—have had this effect: that most people in our times are quite unable even to understand what art is, and accept as art the grossest counterfeits of it.

To what an extent people of our circle and time have

lost the capacity to receive real art, and have become accustomed to accept as art things that have nothing in common with it, is best seen from the works of Richard Wagner, which have latterly come to be more and more esteemed, not only by the Germans, but also by the French and the English, as the very highest art, revealing new horizons to us. Wagner's fundamental thought, as is known, was that the music in an opera should serve poetry, expressing all the shades of a poetical work. This thought is incorrect, because each art has its definite realm, which is not identical with the realm of other arts, but merely comes in contact with them; and therefore, if the manifestation of, I will not say several, but even of two arts—the dramatic and the musical—be united in point of time, as is done in the opera, then the demands of the one art will make it impossible to fulfil the demands of the other. ... In order that a production in the one branch of art should coincide with a production in the other branch, it is necessary that the impossible should happen: that two works from different realms of art should be absolutely exceptional, unlike anything that existed before, and yet should coincide, and be exactly alike. And this cannot be, just as there cannot be two men, or even two leaves on a tree, exactly alike. Still less can two works from different realms of art, the musical and the literary, be absolutely alike.

Wagner's new music lacks the chief characteristic of every true work of art, namely, such entirety and completeness that the smallest alteration in its form would disturb the meaning of the whole work. In a true work of art—poem, drama, picture, song, or symphony—it is impossible to extract one line, one scene, one figure, one bar from its place and put it in another without

ART, FALSE AND TRUE

infringing the significance of the whole work; just as it is impossible, without infringing the life of an organic being, to extract an organ from one place and insert it in another. But in the music of Wagner's last period, with the exception of some parts of little importance which have an independent musical meaning, it is possible to make all kinds of transpositions, putting what was in front behind, and *vice versâ*, without altering the musical sense. And the reason why this does not alter the sense of Wagner's music is because the sense lies in the words and not in the music.

The chief poetical production of Wagner is *The Nibelung's Ring*. . . . It is a model work of counterfeit art, so gross as to be even ridiculous. . . . Of music, *i.e.*, of art serving as a means to transmit a state of mind experienced by the author, there is not even a suggestion. There is something that is absolutely unintelligible musically. In a musical sense a hope is continually experienced, followed by disappointment, as if a musical thought were commenced only to be broken off. If there are something like musical commencements these commencements are so short, so encumbered with complications of harmony and orchestration and with effects of contrast, are so obscure and unfinished, and what is happening on the stage meanwhile is so abominably false, that it is difficult even to perceive these musical snatches, let alone be infected by them. Above all, from the very beginning to the very end, and in each note, the author's purpose is so audible and visible that one sees and hears neither Siegfried nor the birds, but only a limited, self-opinionated German of bad taste and bad style, who has a most savage and rude conception of poetry, and who, in the rudest and most primitive manner, wishes to transmit to us these false and mistaken conceptions of his.

Listening to this opera, I involuntarily thought of a respected, wise, educated country labourer—one, for instance, of those wise and truly religious men whom I know among the peasants—and I pictured to myself the terrible perplexity such a man would be in were he to witness what I was seeing that evening. Not to speak of an adult labourer, one can hardly imagine even a child of over seven occupying himself with such a stupid, incoherent fairy tale. And yet an enormous audience, the cream of the cultured upper classes, sits out six hours of this insane performance, and goes away imagining that by paying tribute to this nonsense it has acquired a fresh right to esteem itself advanced and enlightened. The explanation is that, thanks to his exceptional position in having at his disposal the resources of a king, Wagner was able to command all the methods for counterfeiting art which have been developed by long usage, and that, employing these methods with great ability, he produced a model work of counterfeit art. The reason why I have selected his work for my illustration is that in no other counterfeit of art known to me are all the methods by which art is counterfeited—namely, borrowings, ornaments, effects, and interestingness—so ably and powerfully united.

People say, 'You cannot judge without having seen Wagner performed at Bayreuth: in the dark, where the orchestra is out of sight concealed under the stage, and where the performance is brought to the highest perfection.' . . . Yes, naturally! Only place yourself in such conditions, and you may see what you will. But this can be still more quickly attained by getting drunk or smoking opium. It is the same when listening to an opera of Wagner's. Sit in the dark for four days in company with people who are not quite normal, and, through the auditory nerves, subject your brain to the strongest action of the sounds best adapted to excite it, and you will no doubt be reduced to an abnormal condition and be enchanted by absurdities.

There is one indubitable indication distinguishing real art from its counterfeit, namely, the infectiousness of art. . . . And however poetical, realistic, effectful, or interesting a work may be, it is not a work of art if it does not evoke that feeling (quite distinct from all other feelings) of joy, and of spiritual union with another (the author) and with others (those who are also infected by it). *The stronger the infection the better is the art, as art*, speaking now apart from its subject-matter, *i.e.*, not considering the quality of the feelings it transmits.

And the degree of the infectiousness of art depends on three conditions: (1) on the greater or lesser individuality of the feeling transmitted; (2) on the greater or lesser clearness with which the feeling is transmitted; (3) on the sincerity of the artist, *i.e.*, on the greater or lesser force with which the artist himself feels the emotion he transmits. . . . I have mentioned three conditions of contagiousness in art, but they may all be summed up into one, the last, sincerity, *i.e.*, that the artist should be impelled by an inner need to express his feeling. This condition is always complied with in peasant art, and this explains why such art always acts so powerfully; but it is a condition almost entirely absent from our upper-class art, which is continually produced by artists actuated by personal aims of covetousness or vanity. Thus is art divided from not-art, and thus is the quality of art, as art, decided independently of its subject-matter, *i.e.*, apart from whether the feelings it transmits are good or bad.

How in art are we to decide what is good and what is bad in subject-matter? . . . Art transmitting feelings flowing from the religious perception of our time should be chosen from all the indifferent art, should be acknowledged, highly esteemed and encouraged; while art running counter to that perception should be condemned and despised, and all the remaining indifferent art should neither be distinguished nor encouraged. The religious perception of our time, in its widest and most practical application, is the consciousness that our well-being, both material and spiritual, individual and collective, temporal and eternal, lies in the growth of brotherhood among all men—in their loving harmony with one another.

Christian art, *i.e.*, the art of our time, should be catholic in the original meaning of the word, that is, universal, and therefore it should unite all men. And only two kinds of feeling do unite all men: first, feelings flowing from the perception of their sonship to God and of the brotherhood of man; and next, the simple feelings of common life, accessible to everyone without exception—such as the feeling of merriment, of pity, of cheerfulness, of tranquillity, etc. Only these two kinds of feelings can now supply material for art good in its subject-matter.

If I were asked to give modern examples of each of

these kinds of art—religious and universal—as examples of the highest art, flowing from love of God and man (both of the higher, positive, and of the lower, negative kind), in literature I should name *The Robbers* by Schiller; Victor Hugo's *Les Pauvres Gens* and *Les Misérables;* the novels and stories of Dickens—*The Tale of Two Cities, The Christmas Carol, The Chimes,* and others; *Uncle Tom's Cabin ;* Dostoievsky's works—especially his *Memoirs from the House of Death;* and *Adam Bede*, by George Eliot. In modern painting, strange to say, works of this kind, directly transmitting the Christian feeling of love of God and of one's neighbour, are hardly to be found, especially among the works of the celebrated painters. There are plenty of pictures treating of the Gospel stories; they, however, depict historical events with great wealth of detail, but do not, and can not, transmit religious feeling not possessed by their painters. There are many pictures treating of the personal feelings of various people, but of pictures representing great deeds of self-sacrifice and of Christian love there are very few, and what there are are principally by artists who are not celebrated, and are, for the most part, not pictures but merely sketches.

To give examples, from the modern art of our upper classes, of art of the second kind, good universal art, or even of the art of a whole people, is yet more difficult, especially in literary art and music. If there are some works which by their inner contents might be assigned to this class (such as *Don Quixote,* Molière's comedies, *David Copperfield* and *The Pickwick Papers* by Dickens, Golgol's and Pushkin's tales, and some things of Maupassant's), these works are for the most part—from the exceptional nature of the feelings they transmit, and the superfluity of special details of time and locality, and, above all, on account of the poverty of their subject-matter in comparison with examples of universal ancient art (such, for instance, as the story of Joseph)—comprehensible only to people of their own circle. . . . In music, besides marches and dances by various composers, which satisfy the demand of universal art, one can indicate very few works of this class: Bach's famous violin *aria*, Chopin's nocturne in E flat major, and perhaps a dozen bits (not whole pieces, but parts) selected from the works of Haydn, Mozart, Schubert, Beethoven, and Chopin.

Although in painting the same thing is repeated as in poetry and in music—namely, that in order to make them more interesting, works weak in conception are surrounded by minutely studied accessories of time and place, which give them a temporary and local interest but make them less universal,—still, in painting more than in the other spheres of art may be found works satisfying the demands of universal Christian art; that is to say, there are more works expressing feelings in which all men may participate. In the arts of painting and sculpture, such works, universal in subject-matter, are all pictures and statues in so-called genre style, depictions of animals, landscapes, and caricatures with subjects comprehensible to everyone, and also all kinds of ornaments. Such productions in painting and sculpture are very numerous (*e.g.*, china dolls), but for the most part such objects (for instance, ornaments of all kinds) are not considered to be art.

In the upper classes, in consequence of the loss of capacity to be infected by works of art, people grow up, are educated, and live, lacking the fertilising, improving influence of art, and therefore not only do not advance toward perfection, do not become kinder, but, on the contrary, possessing highly-developed external means of civilisation, they yet become continually more savage, more coarse, and more cruel. Such is the result of the absence from our society of the activity of that essential organ—art.

But the consequences of the perverted activity of that organ are yet more harmful. And they are numerous. The first consequence, plain for all to see, is the enormous expenditure of the labour of working people on things which are not only useless, but which, for the most part, are harmful; and more than that, the waste of priceless human lives on this unnecessary and harmful business. . . . The second consequence is that the productions of amusement-art, which are prepared in such terrific quantities by the armies of professional artists, enable the rich people of our times to live the lives they do, lives not only unnatural, but in contradiction to the humane principles these people themselves profess. To live as do the rich, idle people, especially the women, far from nature and from animals, in artificial conditions, with muscles atrophied or misdeveloped by gymnastics, and with enfeebled vital energy, would be impossible were it not for what is called art—for this occupation and amusement which hides from them the meaninglessness of their lives, and saves them from the dulness that oppresses them. . . . The third consequence of the perversion of art is the perplexity produced in the minds of children and of plain folks. Among people not perverted by the false theories of our society, among workers and children, there exists a very definite conception of what people may be respected and praised for. . . . But these people, children and peasants, suddenly perceive that besides those praised, respected, and rewarded for physical or moral strength, there are others who are praised, extolled, and rewarded much more than the heroes of strength and virtue merely because they sing well, compose verses, or dance. They see that singers, composers, painters, ballet-dancers earn millions of roubles and receive more honour than the saints do; and peasants and children are perplexed. . . . The supplanting of the ideal of what is right by the ideal of what is beautiful, *i.e.*, of what is pleasant, that is the fourth consequence, and a terrible one, of the perversion of art in our society. It is fearful to think of what would befall humanity were such art to spread among the masses of the people. And it already begins to spread. . . . Finally, the fifth and chief result is that the art which flourishes in the upper classes of European society has a directly vitiating influence, infecting people with the worst feelings and with those most harmful to humanity — superstition, patriotism, and, above all, sensuality.

It is not only in Church matters and patriotic matters that art depraves; it is art in our time that serves as the chief cause of the perversion of people in the most important question of social life—in their sexual relations. . . . All art, real and counterfeit, with very few exceptions, is devoted to describing, depicting, and inflaming sexual love in every shape and form. When one remembers all those novels and their lust-kindling descriptions of love, from the most refined to the grossest, with which the literature of our society overflows; if one only remembers all those pictures and statues representing

ART, FALSE AND TRUE

women's naked bodies, and all sorts of abominations which are reproduced in illustrations and advertisements; if one only remembers all the filthy operas and operettas, songs and romances with which our world teems, involuntarily it seems as if existing art had but one definite aim —to disseminate vice as widely as possible. . . . What in our society is called art not only does not conduce to the progress of mankind, but, more than almost anything else, hinders the attainment of goodness in our lives. . . . So that, were the question put: Would it be preferable for our Christian world to be deprived of all that is now esteemed to be art, and, together with the false, to lose all that is good in it? I think that every reasonable and moral man would again decide the question as Plato decided it for his *Republic*, and as all the Church, Christian, and Mohammedan teachers of mankind decided it, *i.e.*, would say, 'Rather let there be no art at all than continue the depraving art, or simulation of art, which now exists.' Happily, no one has to face this question, and no one need adopt either solution.—*What is Art?*

'They played the "Kreutzer Sonata" of Beethoven; do you know the first *presto*? Ah!' he exclaimed, 'it is a strange piece of music, especially the first part of it. And music generally is a strange thing. . . . . They say it acts on one by elevating the soul. That is absurd. It acts upon us, it is true, acts with terrible effect—at least, I am speaking for myself—but it is far from elevating the soul. Music forces me to forget myself and my true state; it transports me to some other state which is not mine. It instantaneously throws me into that state of feeling in which the composer of it found himself when he wrote it. He who composed the piece—Beethoven, for instance, in the case of the "Kreutzer Sonata"—knew perfectly well why he was in that mood; it was that mood that determined him to do certain things, and therefore for him that state of mind has a meaning; for me it has absolutely none. This is why it is that music only causes irritation, never ends anything. It is a different thing if a military march is played, then the soldiers move forward, keeping time to the music, and the end is attained; if dance music is played people dance to it, and the object is also accomplished; if a Mass is sung I receive Holy Communion, and here, too, the music is not in vain; but in other cases there is nothing but irritation, and no light how to act during this irritation. Hence the terrible effects that music occasionally produces. In China music is a State concern, and this is as it ought to be. Could it be tolerated in any county that anyone who takes the fancy may hypnotise anyone else and then do with him whatever he has a mind to, especially if this magnetiser is — Heaven knows who!—an immoral character, for instance? It is indeed a terrible weapon in the hands of those who know how to employ it. Take the "Kreutzer Sonata," for example: is it right to play that first *presto* in a drawing-room to ladies in low dresses? to play that *presto*, then to applaud it, and immediately afterwards to eat ice-creams and discuss the latest scandal? Such pieces as this are only to be executed in rare and solemn circumstances of life, and even then only if certain important deeds that harmonise with this music are to be performed. It is meant to be played and then to be followed by the feats for which it nerves you; but to call into life the energy of a sentiment which is not destined to manifest itself by any deed, how can that be otherwise than baneful?'

'Music—the most refined lust of the senses.'—*The Kreutzer Sonata.*

'The animalism of the brute nature in man is disgusting,' thought Nekhlúdoff, 'but as long as it remains in its naked form we observe it from the height of our spiritual life and despise it; and—whether one has fallen or resisted—one remains what one was before. But when that same animalism hides under a cloak of poetry and æsthetic feeling and demands our worship—then we are swallowed up by it completely, and worship animalism, no longer distinguishing good from evil. Then it is awful.'—*Resurrection.*

In all his novels after *Bel Ami* (I am not now alluding to his short stories, which are his chief merit and glory), Guy de Maupassant has evidently submitted to the theories now reigning, not only in his Parisian circle, but everywhere among artists; theories that, for a work of art, it is not only unnecessary to have any clear conception of what is right and what is wrong, but that, on the contrary, the artist must totally ignore all moral questions, there even being a certain artistic merit in his so doing. . . . In the circle in which Maupassant moved, that beauty which has been, and is, regarded as necessarily to be served by art, is principally woman, young and pretty; and sexual intercourse with her—woman for the most part stripped bare. It was so held, not only by all Maupassant's comrades in 'art,' painters and sculptors, novelists and poets, but also by philosophers, teachers of the rising generation. . . . In the society in which Maupassant grew up and was educated, the representation of feminine beauty and sex-love, quite seriously, as a thing long ago admitted and decided by the cleverest and most learned men, was, and is, regarded as the true object of the highest art, of '*le grand art.*' It is to this very theory, dreadful in its absurdity, that Maupassant subjected himself when he became a fashionable writer. And, as was to be expected, this false ideal led him, in his novels, into a series of mistakes, and into work weaker and more weak.

The astonishing capacity of every man of real genius, if only he does not do violence to himself under the influence of false theory, lies precisely in this: that genius teaches its possessor, leads him forward on the road of moral development, and makes him love that which deserves love, and hate that which deserves hatred. An artist is only an artist because he sees things, not as he wishes to see them, but as they are. With every true artist, when, under the influence of his circle, he begins to represent that which he ought not to represent, there happens what happened to Balaam, who, wishing to bless, cursed what should be cursed, and, wishing to curse, blessed what should be blessed; he will involuntarily do, not what he wishes, but what he should do.

The tragedy of Maupassant's life is that, being in the most monstrous and immoral circle, he, by the force of his genius, that extraordinary light which was in him, struggled out of the views of that circle, and was already near to deliverance, already breathing the air of liberty. But having spent his last force upon this struggle, not able to make one more effort, he perished unfreed. The tragedy of this ruin consists in that it continues even now for the majority of so-called educated men of our time.—*Guy de Maupassant and the Art of Fiction.*

The art of our time and of our circle has become a prostitute. . . . Like her it is not limited to certain times, like her it is always adorned, like her it is always saleable, and like her it is enticing and ruinous.

A real work of art can only arise in the soul of an artist occasionally, as the fruit of the life he has lived—just as a child is conceived by its mother.

Art of the future will consist in transmitting such feelings as embody the highest religious perception of our times. Only those productions will be considered art which transmit feelings drawing men together in brotherly union or such universal feelings as can unite all men. Only such art will be chosen, tolerated, approved, and diffused. But art transmitting feelings flowing from antiquated, worn-out religious teaching—Church art, patriotic art, voluptuous art, transmitting feelings of superstitious fear, of pride, of vanity, of ecstatic admiration of national heroes—art exciting exclusive love of one's own people, or sensuality, will be considered bad, harmful art, and will be censured and despised by public opinion. All the rest of art, transmitting feelings accessible only to a section of people, will be considered unimportant, and will be neither blamed nor praised. And the appraisement of art in general will devolve, not, as is now the case, on a separate class of rich people, but on the whole people.

Artistic activity will then be accessible to all men. It will become accessible to the whole people, because, in the first place, in the art of the future, not only will that complex technique, which deforms the productions of the art of to-day and requires so great an effort and expenditure of time, not be demanded, but, on the contrary, the demand will be for clearness, simplicity, and brevity—conditions mastered not by mechanical exercises but by the education of taste. And secondly, artistic activity will become accessible to all men of the people because, instead of the present professional schools which only some can enter, all will learn music and depictive art (singing and drawing) equally with letters in the elementary schools, and in such a way that every man, having received the first principles of drawing and music, and feeling a capacity for, and a call to, one or other of the arts, will be able to perfect himself in it.

The artist of the future will live the common life of man earning his subsistence by some kind of labour. . . . He will understand that to compose a fairy-tale, a little song which will touch, a lullaby or a riddle which will entertain, a jest which will amuse, or to draw a sketch which will delight dozens of generations or millions of children and adults, is incomparably more important and more fruitful than to compose a novel or a symphony, or paint a picture which will divert some members of the wealthy classes for a short time, and then be for ever forgotten. The art of the future, therefore, will not be poorer, but infinitely richer in subject-matter. And the form of the art of the future will also not be inferior to the present forms of art, but infinitely superior to them. Superior, not in the sense of having a refined and complex technique, but in the sense of the capacity briefly, simply, and clearly to transmit, without any superfluities, the feeling which the artist has experienced and wishes to transmit. . . . And the ideal excellence of the future will not be the exclusiveness of feeling accessible only to some, but, on the contrary, its universality. And not bulkiness, obscurity, and complexity of form . . . but, on the contrary, brevity, clearness, and simplicity of expression.

The task of art is enormous. Through the influence of real art, aided by science, guided by religion, that peaceful co-operation of man which is now obtained by external means—by our law-courts, police, charitable institutions, factory inspection, etc.—should be obtained by man's free and joyous activity. Art should cause violence to be set aside. And it is only art that can accomplish this. . . . The destiny of art in our time is to transmit from the realm of reason to the realm of feeling the truth that well-being for men consists in being united together, and to set up, in place of the existing reign of force, that kingdom of God, *i.e.*, of love, which we all recognise to be the highest aim of humble life.—*What is Art?*

CHAPTER VI

EDUCATION

THERE are no beginners in our school at Yasnaya Polyana. The junior class reads, writes, solves problems in the first three rules of arithmetic, and recites sacred history. The subjects are, accordingly, distributed as follows:—(1) Reading, mechanical and graduated; (2) writing; (3) caligraphy; (4) grammar; (5) sacred history; (6) Russian history; (7) drawing; (8) lineal drawing; (9) singing; (10) mathematics; (11) discourses on natural history; (12) religion. . . . The school occupies a two-storeyed house. Two rooms are taken up by the school, one by the workshop, and two by the teachers. At the entrance, under the fore-roof, there is a bell with a cord tied to its tongue; in the vestibule downstairs, bars and a rake; upstairs, also in the vestibule, a bench-board.

About eight in the morning the teacher, who lives in and manages the school and is a great lover of order and regularity, sends one of the boys that almost invariably stay with him for the night to ring the bell. The people in the village get up while it is yet dark. From the school there have already long been visible lights in the windows, and half an hour after the bell one could see in the mist, in the rain, or in the oblique rays of the autumn sun, dark little figures, in twos or in threes or single,

EDUCATION 227

mounting the hillocks (the village is separated from the school by a ravine). They do not carry anything with them, either books or copy-books; they have no home lessons. Nay, more, they do not even carry anything in their heads. The child is not obliged to remember anything, any lesson that was done yesterday. He is not tormented by the thought of the coming lesson. He brings with him only himself, his receptive mind, and his feeling of certainty that to-day it will be in school just as interesting and cheerful as it was yesterday. He does not think of his class till it actually starts. There is no one to reproach him for his coming late, and there is, in fact, no coming late, unless it be some of the older children whom their fathers sometimes detain at home at some work. And then those big boys come running to the school, almost out of breath. So long as the teacher has not arrived yet, they gather—some of them round the entrance, pushing each other from the steps or sliding on the icy path, and some in the school-rooms. When cold, they read or write or just do something till the teacher comes.

Suppose there is, according to the roster, mechanical reading for the junior standard, graduated reading for the second, and mathematics for the third. The teacher enters the room and sees the children lying in a heap on the floor and screaming, 'Get on the heap!' 'Boys, you're squeezing me to death!' 'Here, that will do; leave my hair!' etc. ... The teacher takes out the books and gives them to those who went with him to the cupboard; those who lie on the top of the heap also ask for books. The heap gradually diminishes. As soon as the majority have taken their books, the rest also run to the cupboard and scream: 'And for me,' 'and for me.'

... The warlike spirit evaporates and the spirit of reading reigns supreme. With the same enthusiasm that he applied to the work of pulling Mitra by the hair he now reads Koltsoff with his teeth nearly set together, with his eyes sparkling, and not seeing anything round but the book. It is just as difficult now to tear him away from his reading as it was before to stop his wrestling.

They sit wherever they like—on the benches, on the tables, on the window-sill, on the floor, and on the armchair. The girls sit always together. Friends from the same village, especially when they are young (there is more comradeship between them), always sit near each other. During the class I have never noticed that the children whisper or pinch each other, or giggle softly, or burst into suppressed laughter, or make complaints of each other to the schoolmaster. The two junior classes are installed in one room, and the senior in the other. The teacher visits also the first class. They gather round him by the side of the blackboard or on the forms, lie or sit on the table round the teacher or one of the readers. If it is a writing lesson, they sit down more quietly, but continually get up from their places to see each other's copy-books or to show theirs to the teacher. It happens sometimes that both the teacher and the scholars are carried away, and then the lesson lasts three hours instead of one. It happens also that the scholars cry out themselves: 'More! more!' and shout down those who are already bored. 'If you are bored you might as well go to the little ones,' they remark contemptuously.

In my opinion, this outward disorder is useful and

EDUCATION

valuable, however strange and inconvenient it may seem to the teacher. . . . It frightens us only because we are used to something quite different . . . and we make use of violence simply in haste and for lack of respect to human nature. It looks to us as if the disorder is on the increase, that it has no limits, that there are no other means of stopping it but by the use of force; but it is only necessary to wait a little and the disorder (or animation) will come to an end, and turn into an order much better and more stable than any which we can think of. Scholars, however young, are still human beings; they all want to learn—that is why they come to school—and they will, therefore, easily come to the conclusion that, in order to learn, they must subject themselves to certain conditions. They are not only human beings, but actually a society of human beings, connected by one and the same thought.

Obeying only natural laws, flowing from their nature, they revolt and grumble when they have to obey your untimely interference. They do not believe in the legality of your bells, rosters, and rules. . . . I have succeeded in discovering among them some rough sense of justice. How often are affairs settled by them by reason of one knows not what law, and yet settled in a manner satisfactory to both parties! How arbitrary and unjust are, in comparison with this, all the education methods in such cases! You just leave them alone, if you are not their father or mother, who simply pity their child, and who, therefore, are always right when pulling by the hair the one who has hit their child. You just leave them, and look how all this is being cleared up and settles down so simply and naturally and, at the same time, so complicatedly and variously, like all other unconscious relations of life. I believe that the school ought not to interfere in the work of education proper, which belongs of right only to the family. The school must not and has no right of meting out rewards or punishments. The best policy and administrative system of a school is to allow the scholars perfect freedom of learning and of governing themselves as they like.

About two, the children, already hungry, run home. In spite of the hunger, they nevertheless wait about for a few moments in order to learn their marks. They are awfully interested in the marks, which, however, carry with them no privileges. . . . However, the system of marks is a mere remnant from our ancient *régime* and is of itself declining. For the first lesson after the dinner interval the scholars gather just as in the morning, and just as then, wait for the teacher. Let us enter the room. It is almost dark behind the frost-covered windows. The elder boys, the best, are pressed by others close to the teacher, and with their little heads raised hang on his lips. The girl of independent character, with her face expressing anxiety, invariably sits on a high table, ready to swallow every word. Smaller children, not so good, sit further in the room: they listen attentively, almost angrily—they behave just like the older ones; but in spite of their attentiveness we know that they will not be able to repeat anything, though they will remember much. Some are leaning on the shoulders of a friend, others simply stand *on* the table. Occasionally someone will get right into the middle of the crowd, behind another's back, and draw with his nail figures on that back. Occasionally somebody will have a look at you. . . . Recently it was the story of the life of our Saviour. . . . Draw closer in the semi-darkness and have a look at some youngster: he sits with his eyes fixed on the teacher and his forehead all in wrinkles of attention. More than once he has already shaken off his shoulder the hand of some leaning comrade. You tickle him in his neck, he will not even smile; he will only jerk his little head as if driving a fly away, and then again yield himself completely to the mysterious and poetical story—how the curtain in the Temple was rent, and darkness enshrouded the earth. And he feels a little frightened, and withal it is pleasant.

Sometimes, when the classes are interesting, and there have been many of them (sometimes seven long hours in a day), and the children are, consequently, tired, or it is the eve of a holiday, when the ovens are being heated at home for a bath, two or three boys would suddenly, without a word, break into the room during the second or third afternoon-lesson and hurriedly take their caps. 'What are you doing?' 'Going home.'

Who are the boys that have decided to go home, and how they took that decision, God alone knows. You will never find out who was the initiator of the step. They held no council, they did not conspire—simply they thought of going home. 'The children are going!' and the little feet pound upon the steps, some jump down in a somersault, and limping and tumbling through the snow the children run home with shouts. Such cases happen once or twice in a week.

In the evening we have singing, graduated reading, discourses, physical experiments, and composition. The most favourite of these subjects are reading and experiments. Usually the classes end by eight or nine in the evening, unless joinery detains the elder boys for some time longer. The entire crowd with shouts run together to the gates and disperse in all directions in groups, shouting to each other.

The opinions of the people about our school have much changed since its establishment. . . . Some, of the richer classes, send their children to school for vanity's sake—to learn 'complete science' and 'division' ('division' is the highest notion of school-wisdom); others think that science is very profitable; whilst the majority simply obey the spirit of the time and send their children to school unconsciously. Of the boys, who form the greater number of our scholars, the most gratifying are exactly those whose fathers belong to the latter category, but who have become so attached to the school that their fathers obey now their wishes and feel instinctively that something good is being done to their boys, and do not dare to take them away from school. The feeling of discontent with the absence of beating and of discipline in the school has almost entirely disappeared, but I have frequently had occasion to see an expression of bewilderment on the face of the parent who came to school to fetch his son when running about and wrestling began in his presence. He is convinced that the lack of order is no good, and at the same time believes that they teach in school well. How both things agree he is unable to comprehend. Gymnastics still give rise to all sorts of rumours, and the superstition that the stomachs are liable on that account to come off still holds the field.

You sit in the school and open a pseudo-popular book and read: 'The life of the great Saint Alexis presents an example of fervid faith, of piety, of incessant activity and of warm attachment to his fatherland, to which he rendered important services. . . .' You give such a book to a boy—the eyes get dim and the boy yawns. . . . The only books that are intelligible to the people, and are to his taste, are not those which have been written for the people, but those written by the people—tales, proverbs, collections of songs, legends, verses, enigmas, etc. . . . Our problem is as follows: for the people to become educated it is necessary to have the opportunity and taste for reading good books, but good books are written in a language which the people does not understand. . . . It is not the word itself that is in the great majority of cases unintelligible; the scholar simply lacks the idea which the word conveys.

The scholars used to write very badly, and the new teacher introduced the method of writing from a copy (a very easy and quiet exercise for the teacher). The scholars felt bored; we were obliged to drop caligraphy, and could not think of any means of improving their handwriting. The elder class themselves discovered that means. On having finished sacred history, the elder boys asked to be allowed to take their copy-books home. The copy-books were dirty, torn, and badly written. R., a very conscientious mathematician, asked for paper and began copying his history. Everyone liked the idea. 'Give me, too, a piece of paper, give me a copy-book'— and all went in for caligraphy, a fashion which lasts in the higher standard even to-day. . . . Almost every one of us, when a small boy, was compelled to use bread at the table—a thing which somehow we did not like. Now we ourselves are fond of eating bread. Almost everyone of us used to be compelled to hold the pen with straightened fingers, but we all held it with fingers crooked, as they were too short. Now, however, we stretch out our fingers. Query: what did they so torment us for when it was bound to happen of itself as soon as it became necessary? Will not this fondness of and demand for knowledge in everything else also come off in time by itself?

In the first and second standards the choice of subjects for composition is left to the scholars themselves. The favourite subjects with these standards is the story of the Old Testament, which they write two months after it has been told to them by the teacher. The same mistake is being committed here as in all other branches of teaching: the teacher thinks the easiest to be the most simple and general, whilst for the scholar the easiest is the complex and vivid. Almost every teacher, being guided by this notion, gives as the subject for the first composition the definition of a table or of a chair, and is unable to perceive that in order to define a table or a chair, one must have attained a high level of philosophical and dialectical development, and that the same scholar who sheds tears over the composition on a chair will excellently depict the feelings of kindness and enmity, the meeting of Joseph with his brothers, or a fight with his chums. As subjects for composition they would naturally select some description of events, their attitude towards some persons, or simply an account of tales heard.

The teacher's chief art in teaching the language and his chief exercise with this end, when he teaches the children to write compositions, is to give proper subjects, and not so much to *give*, but to allow a good choice of those subjects, as well as to fix the size of the composition and to show the first principles of writing it. Every artistic word, whether it belongs to Goethe or to Fedka, differs from an unartistic one solely by the fact that it gives rise to an endless number of thoughts, images, and interpretations.

A healthy child is born into the world, satisfying completely those demands of absolute harmony as regards truth, beauty, and supreme good which we possess within us. . . . At all times and in all countries a child is represented as the embodiment of innocence, purity, truth, beauty, and good. 'Man is born perfect' is a good word spoken by Russians . . . and each subsequent step, each subsequent hour threatens to disturb this harmony and puts off the hope of ever restoring it. . . . *Our ideal is behind us, not before.* Education demoralises men, not corrects. The more a child is demoralised, the less we have to educate him, the more he stands in need of freedom. To teach and educate a child is an impossible and stupid thing, for the simple reason that he stands nearer than I, nearer than all adults, to that ideal of truth, beauty, and good to which I, in my pride, wish to raise him. The consciousness of this ideal is stronger with him than with me. What he requires from me is only material to complete himself harmoniously and thoroughly.—*The School at Fairfield.*

When I reflected I came to the conclusion that what we term education is a deceit. The common people call education fashionable dress, smart conversation, white hands, and a certain degree of cleanliness. Of such a man they say, when distinguishing him from others, that he is an educated man. In a little higher circle, men by education denote the same things, but add playing on the piano, the knowledge of French, good Russian spelling, and still greater cleanliness. In the still higher circle, education consists of all this, with the addition of English, and a diploma from a high Government establishment, and a still greater degree of cleanliness. But in all these shades education is in substance quite the same. It consists in those forms and various kinds of information which separate a man from his fellow-creatures. Its object is the same as that of cleanliness: to separate us from the crowd, in order that they, hungry and cold, may not see how we feast.

We, priests of art and science, are most wretched deceivers, who have much less right to our position than the most cunning and depraved priests ever had. Pagan priests, the clergy, as well Russian as Roman Catholic, however depraved they may have been, had rights to their position, because they professed to teach men about life and salvation. And we, who have cut the ground from under their feet, and proved to men that they were deceivers, we have taken their place, and not only do not teach men about life, we even acknowledge that there is no necessity for them to learn. We suck the blood of the people, and for this we teach our children Greek and Latin grammars in order that they also may continue the same parasitic life which we are living.—*What Then is to be Done?*

We have become so accustomed to the religious lie that surrounds us that we do not notice all the atrocity, stupidity, and cruelty with which the theology of the orthodox Church is permeated. *We* do not notice it, but children do, and their souls are irreparably maimed by this teaching. We have but clearly to understand what we are really doing when we teach children this so-called religion, in order to be appalled by the dreadful crime thus perpetrated. . . . An innocent child inquires about those fundamental truths by which man should be guided in life. We answer his question with a coarse, incoherent, often simply stupid and, above all, cruel Jewish legend, which we repeat either in its original form or, worse still, in our own words. We tell him—assuring him that this is the sacred truth—that which, as we are well aware, is impossible, and has for us no meaning. . . . We imagine there is no harm in this, and even that it is useful to the child; and we listen with pleasure as he repeats all these horrors, and do not realise the dreadful distortion—imperceptible to us because it is spiritual—that is thereby taking place in the child's soul. 'We think that the soul of a child is a clear board on which we may write all we choose. But this is not the case. The child has a vague consciousness of the cause of his existence, its object, and the duties of man. . . . It seems unimportant to us, and yet the teaching to children of this so-called religion which is taking place among us is the most dreadful crime we can possibly imagine. Torture, murder, the violation of children are nothing in comparison with this crime.

The Government, the ruling classes, those in power, stand in need of this fraud. Whereas those who desire, not the maintenance of the present false social organisation, but, on the contrary, its reform, and, above all, those who desire the welfare of the children with whom they come in contact, should endeavour with all their might to deliver children from this dreadful fraud.

If I now had to transmit to a child the substance of

the religious teaching I consider true, I should say to him that we have come into this world and live in it, not according to our own will, but according to the will of that which we call God, and that it will, therefore, be well with us only when we fulfil this will. This will is that we should all be happy; and for all to be happy there is but one means: each must act towards others as he would wish that they should act towards him. As to the questions about how the world came into existence, and what awaits us after death, I would answer to the first by the acknowledgment of my ignorance, and of the anomaly of such a question (in all the Buddhist world no such question exists); and to the second I would answer by the conjecture that the will of Him who called us into this life for our welfare leads us somewhere through death—probably for the same purpose.—*The Religious Education of the Young*.

CHAPTER VII

RELIGION

I.—The New Life-Conception

The birth of the life-conception, which always takes place when mankind enters upon new conditions, and its subsequent activities, is what we call religion. Religion is not, as science regards it, a phenomenon which formerly travelled hand in hand with the development of mankind, and which has since been left behind; on the contrary, it is a phenomenon inherent to human existence itself, and never more distinctly manifested than at the present day. In the second place, religion defines future rather than past activities, therefore it is evident that an investigation of the phenomena of the past can by no means touch the essence of religion. The longing to typify the forces of nature is no more the essence of religion than is the fear of those same forces, or the need of the miraculous and its outward manifestations, as the scientists suppose. The essence of religion lies in the power of man to foreknow and to point out the way in which mankind must walk. It is a definition of a new life which will give birth to new activities. This faculty of foreknowledge concerning the density of humanity is more or less common, no doubt, to all people; still from time to time a man appears in whom the faculty has reached a higher development, and these men have the power clearly and distinctly to formulate that which is vaguely conceived by all men, thus instituting a new life-conception from which is to flow an unwonted activity, whose results will endure for centuries to come.

Thus far there have been three of these life-conceptions; two of them belong to a bygone era, while the third is of our own time and is called Christianity. It is not that we have merged the various conceptions of the significance of life into three arbitrary divisions, but that there really have been but three distinct conceptions, by which the actions of mankind have been influenced, and save through these we have no means of comprehending life. These three life-conceptions are—firstly, the individual or animal; secondly, the social or pagan; and thirdly, the universal or divine. According to the first of these, a man's life is his personality, and that only, and his life's object is to gratify his desires. According to the second, his life is not limited to his own personality; it includes the sum and continuity of many personalities—of the family, of the race, and of the State, and his life's object is to gratify the will of the communities of individuals. And according to the third his life is confined neither to his personality nor to that of the aggregate of individuals, but finds its significance in the eternal source of all life—in God Himself. These three life-conceptions serve as the basis for the religions of every age. . . . History is but the transcript of the gradual transition from the animal life-conception of the individual to the social, and from the social to the divine. The history of the ancients for thousands of centuries, culminating in that of Rome, is the history of the evolution from the animal life-conception of the

THE NEW LIFE-CONCEPTION 241

individual to that of society and the State. From the advent of Christianity and the fall of Imperial Rome, we have the history of that change which is still going on from the social to the divine life-conception.

The distinction between the Christian doctrine and those which preceded it may be thus defined. The social doctrine says: Curb thy nature (meaning the animal nature alone), subject it to the visible law of the family, of society, and of the State. Christianity says: Live up to thy nature (meaning the divine nature); make it subject to nothing, neither to thine own animal nature, nor to that of another, and then thou shalt attain what thou seekest by subjecting thine outward personality to visible laws. The Christian doctrine restores to man his original consciousness of self, not the animal self, but the God-like self, the spark of divinity, as the son of God, like unto the Father, but clothed in a human form. This consciousness of oneself as a son of God, whose essence is love, satisfies at once all those demands made by the man who professes the social life-conception for a broader sphere of love. Again, in the social life-conception, the enlargement of the domain of love was a necessity for the salvation of the individual; it was attached to certain objects, to oneself, to one's family, to society, and to humanity. With the Christian world-conception love is not a necessity, neither is it attached to any special object; it is the inherent quality of a man's soul; he loves because he cannot help loving. The Christian doctrine teaches to man that the essence of his soul is love; that his well-being may be traced, not to the fact that he loves this object or that one, but to the fact that he loves the principle of all things—God, whom he recognises in himself through love, and will by the love of God love all men and all things.

The principal reason of all the misconceptions of the teaching of Christ is that men look upon it as one that may be accepted or rejected without any special change in one's life. . . . The universal brotherhood of man, the equality of races, the abolition of property, the anomalous doctrine of non-resistance, all these requirements of the Christian religion seem to us impossibilities. But in olden times, thousands of years ago, not only the requirements of the State, but even those of the family, as, for instance, the obligation of parents to feed their children, of children to support their aged parents, and that of conjugal fidelity, seemed equally impossible. And still more unreasonable seemed the demands of the State, requiring citizens to submit to established authority, to pay taxes, to perform military duty in defence of their country, etc. . . . The time will come, and it is already near at hand, when the Christian foundations of life—equality, brotherly love, community of goods, non-resistance of evil by violence—will seem as natural and simple as the foundations of family, social, and State life appear to us at the present time.—*The Kingdom of God is Within You.*

To understand philosophy and science one needs study and preparation, but neither is required for the understanding of religion. . . . An almost illiterate sectarian peasant in Russia, without the slightest mental effort, achieves the same conception of life as was accomplished by the greatest sages of the world. You may ask : In what, then, does the essence of this unscientific and unphilosophical knowledge consist ? I can only reply that as religious knowledge is that which precedes, and upon which is founded, every other knowledge, it cannot be defined, there being no means of definition in existence. In theological language this knowledge is called revelation. And this word, if we do not give it any mystic meaning, is quite accurate, because this knowledge is not acquired by study, nor by the efforts of individuals, but through the reception by them of the manifestation of the Infinite Mind, which little by little discloses itself to men. . . . The qualities which give to some the power of receiving the rising truth are no special activities of the mind, but, on the contrary, are rather passive qualities of the heart, seldom corresponding to a great and inquisitive intellect. Rejection of the vanities of the world, a sense of one's material frailty, and of truthfulness, are what we observe in every founder of a religion, none of whom have been distinguished by philosophical or scientific acquirement.

So I answer your first question, as to what I understand by the word 'religion,' thus—Religion is a certain relation of man to the eternal, infinite universe, its origin and source. Out of this reply to your first question follows naturally that to the second. If religion is a definite relation of man to the universe which determines the meaning of his life, morality is the index and explanation of man's activity which naturally flows from one or other perceived relation. And as we recognise only two of these perceptions, if we include the pagan-social as the enlargement of the personal relation, or three, if we consider it apart, so there exist *but three moral teachings: the primitive, savage, individualistic; the pagan-family-State or social; and the Christian or godly, teaching man's subservience to the universe or to God.*

At the present time most men only imagine they profess Christianity and hold the Christian morality, but in reality they follow this family-State morality of paganism. But it is from the third conception of man's relation to the universe that there arises the loftiest morality known to man—the Pythagorean, Stoic, Buddhist, Brahmin, and Taoist in their best aspects, and the Christian teaching in its real sense, which demands the *renunciation of the individual will, and of the welfare, not only of the individual, but of family, society, and State, in the name of the fulfilment of His will who gave us the existence which our consciousness has disclosed.*—*Religion and Morality.*

II.—THE PLACE OF ETHICS

Morality is included in the explanation of life which religion offers us and therefore cannot possibly be divorced from it. . . . Huxley tries to prove that the struggle for existence does not violate morality, and that, alongside the acceptance of the law of this struggle as the fundamental law of existence, morality may not only exist, but may improve. Mr Huxley's article is full of a variety of jokes, verses, and general views upon the religion and philosophy of the ancients, and therefore is so shock-headed and entangled that only with great pains can one arrive at the fundamental idea. . . . Social progress exists which tends to suspend the cosmic process and to replace it by another—an ethical one, the object of which is no longer the survival of the 'fittest,' but of the 'best' in the ethical sense. Whence came this ethical process Mr Huxley does not explain. . . . To assert that social progress produces morality is equivalent to saying that the erection of stoves produces heat. Morality proceeds from religion, and social forms of life produce morality only when into these forms are put the results of religious influence on humanity. . . . Ethical treatises not founded on religion, only try to counterfeit the natural outflux of religion. Ordinances of lay morality not founded upon religious teaching are similar to the actions of a man who, being ignorant of music, should take the conductor's seat before the orchestra, and begin to wave his arms before the musicians who are performing. The music might continue a little while by its own momentum, and from the previous knowledge of the players, but it is evident that the mere waving of a stick by a man who is ignorant of music would not only be useless, but would inevitably confuse the musicians and disorganise the orchestra in the end. The same disorder is beginning to take place in the minds of the men of our time, in consequence of the attempts of leading men to teach people morality not founded on that loftiest religion which is in process of adoption, and is in part adopted by Christian humanity. . . . The attempts to found a morality independent of religion are like the actions of children when, wishing to move a plant which pleases them, they tear off the root which does not please and seems unnecessary to them, and plant it in the earth without the root. Without a religious foundation there can be no true, unsimulated morality, as without a root there can be no true plant.—*Religion and Morality.*

It is true that, on the one hand, man is an animal and cannot cease to be an animal while he lives in the flesh; but, on the other hand, he is a spiritual being, rejecting all the demands of the animal in man. During the first period of his life man lives without consciousness of living; hence it is not he that lives, but through him lives that power of life which lives in all we know. Man only begins to live himself when he becomes conscious that he lives. He becomes conscious that he lives when he knows that he desires welfare for himself and that other beings have the same desire. This knowledge is given him by the awakening in him of reason. Having found out that he lives and desires welfare for himself, and that other beings have the same desire, man inevitably also discovers that the welfare he desires for his own separate being is unattainable, and that, instead of the welfare he desires, unavoidable suffering and death are awaiting him. Man desires to be either a beast or an angel, but he can be neither the one nor the other. And here we come to the solution of this contradiction given by the Christian teaching. It tells man that he is neither a beast nor an angel, but an angel being born of a beast—a spiritual existence being born of an animal one—and that all our life in this world is naught else but this process of birth.

As soon as man is born to reasonable consciousness this consciousness tells him that he desires welfare; and his reasonable consciousness being born in his separate being, it seems to him that his desire for welfare relates to that separate being. But that same reasonable consciousness which showed him himself as a separate being desiring welfare for himself, shows him also that this separate being is incompatible with that desire for welfare and life with which he associates it. He sees that this separate being can have neither welfare nor life. 'What, then, constitutes true life?' he asks himself; and he perceives that there is true life neither in himself nor in those beings that surround him, but only in that which desires welfare. And, having discovered this, man ceases to regard his own isolated bodily and mortal being as himself, but regards as himself that being (inseparable from others, spiritual, and therefore not mortal) which is disclosed to him by his reasonable consciousness. This constitutes the birth in man of the new spiritual being.

The clearer and firmer reason becomes the more clearly it appears, as soon as he is conscious of himself, that the true *self* of man is not his body (which is devoid of true life), but this very desire for welfare—the desire for the welfare of all that exists, *i.e.*, universal welfare. The desire for universal welfare is that which gives life to all that does exist; it is that which we call God. So that the being disclosed to man in his consciousness, this being that is coming to life, that which gives life to all that exists, is God.—*The Christian Teaching*.

III.—God

God is for me that after which I strive—that in striving after which consists my life, and who therefore for me *is;* but is necessarily such that I cannot comprehend or name Him. If I understood Him, I should have reached Him, and there would be nothing to strive after; there would be no life. But all this seems a contradiction: though I cannot understand nor name Him, yet at the same time I know Him and the direction towards Him, and even of all my knowledge this is the most certain. . . . What is still more strange is that to know Him more and better than I do at present is not my desire now in this present life, and is not necessary. . . . I have only to add that the pronoun 'He' somewhat destroys my idea of God, somewhat diminishes Him.

God is All, that infinite All of which I am conscious of being a part, and therefore all in me is encompassed by God, and I feel Him in everything. . . . Somehow, while praying to God, it became clear to me that God is indeed a real Being, Love—is that All which I just touch, and which I experience in the form of love.

One should do as the Spirit-Wrestlers do—bow down to the ground before every man, remembering that in him is God. If to bow physically is impracticable, we should at all events do so spiritually.

This is what has happened to me: I began to think more and more abstractly about the problems of life. . . . And the Devil ensnared me, and it began to enter my mind that it is possible, and especially desirable for union with the Chinese Confucians, with the Buddhists, and our own atheists and agnostics, altogether to avoid this conception. I thought it was possible to restrict oneself to the conception and acknowledgment of that God only which is in me, without acknowledging any God apart from that—without acknowledging the one who has implanted in me a particle of Himself. And, strange to say, I suddenly began to feel dull, depressed, and alarmed. I did not know the cause of this, but I felt that I had suddenly undergone a dreadful spiritual fall, had lost all spiritual joy and energy. And then only did I comprehend that this had happened because I had deserted God. And I began to think, and, strange to say, to guess whether there be a God or not; and I found Him, as it were, afresh. . . . It is as if I had been within a hair's-breadth of losing, nay, had thought that I had actually lost, the Being dearest to me; and yet had not so lost Him but had only realised His priceless worth. . . . Perhaps this is what some call the 'living God'; if that be so, then I did very wrongly towards them in not agreeing with but contradicting them.

There is not one believing man to whom moments of doubt do not come—doubt of the existence of God. And these doubts are not harmful; on the contrary, they lead to a higher understanding of God. We entirely believe in God only when He discloses Himself afresh to us.

One should never go to God, as it were, 'on purpose.' Coming to God is something like getting married: one should do it only when one would be glad not to come to Him, or not to get married, but cannot help doing so. Not that I would tell a man: 'Go purposely into temptations'; but to him who formulates the question thus: 'Well, and is it certain that I will not lose by going to God instead of to the devil?'—I would cry out as loud as I can, 'Go, go to the devil, by all means to the devil!' It is a hundred times better to get well scalded against the devil than to keep on standing at the cross roads, or insincerely going to God.

One of the superstitions that most confuse our metaphysical conceptions is the superstition that the world was created, that it arose out of nothing, and that there is a God-Creator. In reality we have no ground for imagining a God-Creator, nor any necessity. A Creator, a Providence, is incompatible with the Christian God-

Father, God-Spirit. The God who is Love, a particle of whom lives in me, constitutes my life; and the manifestation and avocation of this particle constitutes the meaning of my life. God the Creator is indifferent, and allows suffering and evil. God the Spirit delivers from suffering and evil, and is always perfect welfare.

The moral law, being founded on phenomena of life, will always be local, temporary, casual, and, above all, doubtful. . . . No temporary law, not founded upon the relation to the infinite, can ever be certain. Only such a relation to the Universe, to God, as gives a certain continual direction of conduct can be the basis of morality.

Nothing better proves the existence of God than the attempts of the evolutionists to accept morality and deduce it from the struggle for existence . . . to admit in the form of morality that same God whom they have excluded from their view of life. The other day a Frenchman asked me, 'Would it not be sufficient to base morality upon righteousness and beauty?'—again that same God whom they are afraid to name.

I like to address God. If there were no God, the call into empty space were in itself good. From such an appeal, all those weaknesses of vanity, self-complacency, self-interest, from which it is hardly possible to be free when appealing to men, are absent. So help me, Father!

It is said that God should be conceived as a personality. This is a great misunderstanding; personality is limitation. Man feels himself a personality only because he is in contact with other personalities. If he were alone, he would not be a person. These two conceptions—the external world (other beings), and our own personality—mutually define one another. If there were not the world of other beings, man would not be conscious of his own personality, nor realise the possibility of the existence of other beings. And therefore a man in the world cannot conceive himself otherwise than as a person. But how can we say of God that He is a person? Herein lies the root of anthropomorphism. We can only say of God that which Mahomet and Moses said: that 'He is One.' But there can be no notion of number in relation to God, therefore this implies not that He is one numerically, but that He is one-centred: not a conception, but a being, that which the orthodox call 'the living God' in contrast to the pantheistic God; that is, the highest spiritual being who lives in all. He *is* one in the sense that He exists as a being who can be addressed; that is, that there is a relation between me, a limited personality, and God, unfathomable but existing. We know God as a single being, we cannot know Him otherwise, and yet we cannot realise one single being as pervading all. In this we find the chief incomprehensibleness of God. If God be not One, then He becomes diffused, non-existent, whereas if He be One, then we involuntarily represent Him to ourselves as a personality, and He is no longer the Higher Being, the All. And, nevertheless, to know God, to lean on Him, we are forced to conceive Him both as pervading all, and at the same time as One.—*Thoughts on God.*

IV.—SINS AND SNARES

The obstacles that hinder the manifestation of love by man are (1) his body—its separateness from other beings—and (2) the fact that, beginning his life with infancy, during which period he lives only for the animal life of his separate being, he cannot later on, even when reason is awakened, altogether disentangle himself from desiring the welfare of his separate being, and so commits acts opposed to love. Love, the desire for universal welfare, in its efforts towards its own manifestation, meets with obstacles in man's body largely because reason, which sets love free, wakes in man, not at his first appearance on earth, but considerably later, when he has already developed habits of animal life.

For the solution of the contradiction of life, according to the Christian teaching, it is necessary neither to destroy the life of the separate being (which would be contrary to the will of God, who has sent it), nor to submit to the demands of the animal life of the separate being, *i.e.*, to act in opposition to the spiritual element which constitutes the true 'self' of man; but in that body which encloses the true self of man to serve God alone. The true 'self' of man, the infinite love which lives within him, always tending to increase, and constituting the essence of his life, is enclosed within the limits of the animal life of the separate being and tends always to liberate itself from it. This liberation of the spiritual being from the animal individuality, this birth of the spiritual being, constitutes the true life of man, individual and collective. Love in every separate man and in all mankind is like steam confined in a boiler; the steam expands, drives the pistons, and performs the work. As, in order that the steam may do its work, there must be the resistance of the boiler, so also, that love may accomplish its work, there must be the resistance caused by the limits of the separate being which encloses it.

Having in childhood acquired habits connected with the personal life of his separate being, and having also these same habits of personal life transmitted to him by tradition from his ancestors, every man is always liable to sins, obstacles to the manifestation of love.* There are three kinds of sins:—(*a*) Sins which proceed from the ineradicable tendency of man towards his own personal welfare while living in the body—*innate, natural* sins. (*b*) Sins which proceed from the traditions of the institutions and customs directed to the increase of the welfare of separate persons—*traditional, social* sins. (*c*) Sins which proceed from the tendency of individual man towards the greater and greater augmentation of the welfare of his separate being—*personal, artificial* sins.

There are six sins or obstacles to the manifestation of love in man: (*a*) The *sensual* sin, which consists in preparing for oneself pleasure by the satisfaction of one's needs. (*b*) The sin of *idleness*, which consists in liberating oneself from the labour necessary to the satisfaction of one's needs. (*c*) The sin of *avarice*, which consists in acquiring for oneself power to satisfy one's needs in the future. (*d*) The sin of *ambition*, which consists in subjugating to oneself one's fellow-creatures. (*e*) The *sexual* sin, which consists in arranging for oneself pleasure from sexual instinct. (*f*) The sin of *intoxication*, which consists in producing

* The translator points out that Tolstoy uses words such as *sin, snare, prayer*, etc., not in the conventional orthodox sense, but in a sense which he usually defines at the outset, and adheres to.

artificial excitement of one's physical and mental faculties.

When a man eats or drinks, not being hungry; when he dresses, not for the purpose of protecting his body from the cold; when he builds a house, not for the purpose of sheltering himself from the weather; but does these things in order to increase the pleasure arising from satisfying his needs, he commits innate sensual sin. When a man who has been born and bred in habits of superfluity in drink, food, dress, and lodging, continues to maintain these habits and to profit by the superfluity he possesses, such a man commits traditional sensual sin. When a man, already living in luxury, invents additional, new, and pleasanter means of satisfying his needs, such as are not used by those around him; when he introduces new and more refined foods and drinks in place of his former simple fare, new, finer clothing in place of the former clothing which sufficed to cover his body; builds another house with new adornments in place of the former small, simple one—and so on, such a man commits personal sensual sin.

The fact that a man cannot do everything for himself, and that division of labour often improves and facilitates work, cannot justify a man in liberating himself either from work in general, or from heavy work in favour of light work. Every product of labour which a man uses demands corresponding labour from him, not mitigation of his labour, nor complete liberation from it. The sin of idleness, innate, traditional, or personal, consists in man relinquishing his own work and profiting by the labour of others, the reverse of what he was intended to do, since true welfare is obtained only by service of others. Besides, the man who acts thus fails to obtain even that pleasure which he seeks, as, the enjoyment of rest being attained only after work, the less work the less enjoyment from rest.

The instinct of the continuation of the race—the sexual instinct—is innate in man. In the animal condition he fulfils his destiny by satisfying this instinct, and in so fulfilling it finds welfare. But with the awakening of consciousness it appears to man that the gratification of this instinct may increase the welfare of his separate being; and he enters into sexual intercourse, not with the object of continuing the race, but to increase his personal welfare. This constitutes the sexual sin. The sexual sin differs from all others in this respect: that whereas in other cases a complete abstinence from innate sin is impossible and only a diminution is attainable, complete abstinence from the sexual sin is possible. This is so because entire abstinence from the satisfaction of personal needs—food, clothing, shelter—would destroy the individual, as would also deprivation of all rest, all property, all struggle; but abstinence from satisfying the sexual instinct does not destroy the individual. The abstinence of one, several, or many persons from sexual intercourse would not end the race, to perpetuate which is the object of the sexual instinct. So that satisfaction of this instinct is not obligatory upon every man; but to each individual is left the possibility of abstaining from it.

Man is, as it were, allowed the choice between two ways of serving God: either, by keeping free from married life and its consequences, he may by his own life in this world himself fulfil all that God has appointed to be fulfilled by man; or else, conscious of his own weakness, he may transmit to the posterity he has begotten, nourished and brought up, the fulfilment, or at least the possibility of fulfilment, of that which he has himself neglected. The sexual sin, *i.e.*, mistake, for the man who has chosen the service of chastity, consists in this: he might have chosen the highest vocation and used all his powers in the service of God, and, consequently, for the spread of love and towards the attainment of the highest welfare, instead of which he descends to a lower plane of life and deprives himself of this welfare. The sexual sin or mistake for the man who has chosen to continue the race will consist in the fact that by depriving himself of having children, or, at all events, of family relationships, he deprives himself of the highest welfare of sexual life. In addition to this—as with the gratification of all needs—those who try to increase the pleasure of sexual intercourse diminish the natural pleasure in proportion as they addict themselves to lust.

But for the sin of idleness, one would not on the one hand see men exhausted by overwork, and on the other vitiated by inaction and constant amusement; men would not be divided into two hostile camps—the surfeited and the famished, the festive and the overburdened. Were there no sin of avarice, there would be none of that violence which is committed for the sake of acquiring and retaining property; there would be no theft, robbery, and consequent imprisonment, exile, penal servitude, executions. Were there no sin of ambition, there would be none of that enormous and useless expenditure of human energy for the purpose of subduing others and of maintaining power; there would be neither the arrogance and heartlessness of the conqueror, nor the obsequiousness, deceit, and hatred of the conquered; there would be no family, social, and national divisions, nor the quarrels, fights, murders, and wars arising from them.

Notwithstanding prohibitions and punishments, men have continued, and still continue, to sin, destroying their own lives and those of their fellows. This arises from the fact that for the justification of sins there exist false arguments, according to which there would appear to be exceptional circumstances rendering sins not only excusable but even necessary. These false justifications may be called 'snares.' A snare (Greek, '*scandalos*') signifies a trap; and, indeed, a moral snare is a trap, into which a man is enticed by the similitude of good, and in which, when caught, he perishes. . . . From the time when the contradiction between the animal and the spiritual life was revealed to man, from the time when man began to commit sins, he began also to devise justifications of sins—*i.e.*, snares. There have, therefore, been established among men identical traditional justifications or snares; so that a man need not himself devise justifications for his sins, for the snares are already invented and he has but to accept them ready-made.

There are five snares which ruin men: the personal snare, or snare of preparation; the family snare, or snare of the continuation of the race; the snare of activity, or utility; the snare of fellowship, or fidelity; and the State snare, or snare of the general good. The personal snare, or snare of preparation, consists in man, while committing sins, justifying himself by the consideration that he is preparing for an activity which will be useful to him in the future. The family snare, or snare of the continuation of the race, consists in a man justifying himself on the ground of his children's welfare. The snare of activity, or utility, consists in a man justifying his sins by urging the necessity of continuing or completing some work, already begun, which shall be useful to men. The snare of fellowship, or fidelity, consists in the justification of man's sins by the consideration of the welfare of those with whom he is in some special relationship. The State snare, or snare of the general good, consists in men justifying the sins they commit by the consideration of the welfare of a number of people, of a nation, of humanity. This snare was expressed by Caiaphas, when he demanded the execution of Christ in the name of the welfare of many.

Were it not for the snares of preparation, the family activity, and the State, no one, however cruel, would be able, surrounded by men dying of starvation, to profit by those superfluities which the rich now enjoy; and the rich could never reach that condition of complete physical idleness in which they now spend their dreary lives, often compelling the old, the infirm, and children to perform the work they require done. If it were not for these snares, which justify property, men could not senselessly and aimlessly spend all their vital powers in accumulating property which cannot be used; neither could they, while suffering from the results of strife, call it forth in others. But for the snare of fellowship there would not be a tithe of the depravity that now exists, nor could people so obviously and foolishly destroy their mental and physical powers by intoxication, which diminishes, instead of increasing, their energy. To snares are due the permanence and sanctification of sin—the legalisation of the destitution and oppression of some and of the opulence and idleness of others, the legalisation of violence, murder, war, depravity, intoxication—and the awful stage of development to which these evils have now attained.

Having freed himself from the deception inculcated in childhood, avoided that of impressive ceremonies, and rejected all intermediaries between himself and God, man will not yet be free from religious deception and capable of understanding Christ's teaching unless he liberate himself from faith in the supernatural, the miraculous. It is said that miracles, *i.e.*, the supernatural, are performed with the object of uniting men; but, in fact, nothing so disunites them, for every religion has its own miracles and repudiates those of all others. Nor can this be otherwise. The miraculous or supernatural is infinitely various; the natural only is everywhere and always the same. So, to escape the deception of faith in the miraculous, man must acknowledge as true only that which is natural, which is in accordance with his reason, and must recognise as false all that is unnatural—that contradicts his reason—knowing that all that is given out as such is human deception, as are various contemporary miracles, cures, raisings of the dead, miraculous images, relics, the transformation of bread and wine, etc., and as are the miracles related in the Bible, the Gospels, and in the Buddhist, Mohammedan, Laotzian, and other Scriptures.

Though freed from religious deception, and understanding Christ's teaching, man is always in danger of falling into snares. The essence of all snares consists in this: that having awakened to consciousness, man experiences the discord and suffering caused by sin, and seeks to escape both, not by striving against the sin, but by justifying it. So, to escape snares, man must, above all, avoid lying, especially to himself; being careful not so much to abstain from lying before others as to himself, *i.e.*, not hiding from himself the motive of his actions.

There is a connection and sequence between sins by which one sin engenders others, or hinders liberation from them. Man cannot liberate himself from any sins so long as he addicts himself to the sin of intoxication; he cannot liberate himself from the sin of ambition if he yield to that of avarice, or from avarice while he is addicted to the sin of idleness; he cannot free himself from sexual sin if he addict himself to sensual sin and that of idleness; and he cannot liberate himself from ambition and avarice so long as he yields to sensual sin. This does not mean that one should not strive against every sin at all times, but that for success in the contest one should know with which to begin, or rather with which one cannot begin. It is often only this striving against sins in the wrong order which causes that want of success which drives men to despair.

It is only after having liberated himself from these sins—after having ceased to invent new means of augmenting his personal welfare—that man can begin to contend against the habits and traditions of sin established in his particular circle. And only when he has conquered these traditional sins can a man begin to strive against innate ones.

The reason of men educated in human society is in truth never free from perversion, for every man so educated inevitably undergoes the perversion of religious deception. This deception consists in men of former generations instilling into succeeding ones by various artificial means an understanding of the meaning of life founded, not upon reason, but upon blind confidence. The essence of religious deception is the intentional confusion of faith and credulity, and the substitution of one for the other.

Truth needs no external corroboration, being freely accepted by all to whom it is transmitted; but falsehood demands special methods by which it may be transmitted to men and adopted by them; and the same methods to achieve this end have always been made use of by men. There are five such methods: (1) The misinterpretation of truth—to verbally acknowledge the teaching and even deify the teacher, and at the same time to conceal the essence of the truth so that it may confirm the old order of life; (2) faith in the miraculous; (3) the institution of intermediaries between God and man; (4) influence exerted upon man's senses; (5) the inculcation of erroneous faith into children.

Sin, causing man to at times commit acts contrary to his spiritual nature—to love—impedes his birth to the new true life. Snares, by justifying sins, lead man into a life of sin; so that he not only commits certain sinful acts, but, while living an animal life, does not perceive it to be in contradiction to the true life. Such a position is possible only when the truth is perverted by religious deception. No man whose understanding is not thus perverted can be blind to the falsehood of snares. Religious deception is, therefore, the foundation of all sins and calamities of mankind. Religious deception is that which is called in the Gospel 'blasphemy against the Holy Ghost,' concerning which it is said that it cannot be pardoned, *i.e.*, it can never, in any life, fail to be ruinous.

In order to live according to the teaching of Christ, man must first of all free himself from religious deception. Only after having freed himself from this can a man liberate himself from the falsehood of snares; only after seeing the falsehood of snares can he free himself from sins.—*The Christian Teaching.*

V.—Scripture, the Church, Prayer

Young men, and men of the people, doubting the truth of the Church teaching in which they have been brought up, often come to me and ask what 'my' teaching is, and how 'I' understand Christ's teaching. Such questions always grieve, and even shock me. Christ, who the Churches say was God, came on earth to reveal divine truth to men, for their guidance in life. A man —even a plain, stupid man—if he wants to give people guidance of importance to them, will manage to impart it so that they can make out what he means. And is it possible that God, having come on earth specially to save people, was not able to say what He wanted to say clearly enough to prevent people from misinterpreting His words, and from disagreeing with each other about them? This could not be so if Christ were God; nor even if Christ were not God, but merely a great teacher, is it possible that He failed to express himself clearly. For a great teacher is great just because he is able to express the truth so that it can neither be hidden nor obscured, but is as plain as daylight. In either case, therefore, the Gospels which transmit Christ's teaching must contain truth. And, indeed, the truth is there for all who will read the Gospels with a sincere wish to know the truth, without prejudice, and, above all, without supposing that the Gospels contain some special sort of wisdom beyond human reason. That is how I read the Gospels, and I found in them truth plain enough for little children to understand, as, indeed, is said in the Gospels. So that when I am asked what 'my' teaching consists in, and how I understand Christ's teaching, I reply: I have no teaching, but I understand Christ's teaching as it is explained in the Gospels. If I have written books about Christ's teaching, I have done so only to show the falseness of the interpretations given by the commentators on the Gospels.

To understand any book one must choose out the parts that are quite clear, dividing them from what is obscure or confused. And from what is clear we must form our idea of the drift and spirit of the whole work. Then, on the basis of what we have understood, we may proceed to make out what is confused or not quite intelligible. It is particularly necessary thus to read the Gospels, which have passed through such a multiplicity of compilations, translations, and transcriptions, and were composed, eighteen centuries ago, by men who were not highly educated, and were superstitious. . . . We know how these works were written and collected, and how they were corrected and translated; and therefore not only can we not accept them as infallible revelations, but we must, if we respect truth, correct errors that we find in them.—*How to read the Gospels.*

In no place, and in no manner whatsoever, save in the assertion of the Church, is it seen that either God or Christ can ever have founded anything like the Church in its ecclesiastical sense. . . . There is but one exact definition of what is called a Church (not the imaginary Church which we may desire, but the actual Church which has really existed). The Church is a body of men which lays claim to the exclusive possession of the truth. . . . But to claim for one's self, or for any body of men whatsoever, the possession of a complete apprehension and practice of the doctrine of Christ is in direct contradiction to the spirit of Christ's doctrine itself.

However strange the statement may appear, every Church, as a Church, has always been, and always must be, an institution not only foreign, but absolutely hostile to the doctrine of Christ. It is not without reason that Voltaire called it '*l'infâme*'; it is not without reason that all so-called sectarians believe the Church to be the Scarlet Woman prophesied by the Revelation; it is not without reason that the history of the Church is the history of cruelties and horrors. Between Churches in the ecclesiastical sense and Christianity, not only is there nothing in common except the name, but they are two utterly contradictory and hostile elements. One is pride, violence, self-assertion, inertia, and death. The other is meekness, repentance, submission, activity, and life.

The people are coming to recognise the moral, vital side of Christianity more and more plainly. . . . Let the Church but pause in its effort to influence the masses by hypnotising men and deceiving children for ever so short a time, and men will comprehend the doctrine of Christ, and this comprehension will do away with Churches and their influence.—*The Kingdom of God is Within You.*

People who believe in the spiritual life, in their spiritual essence, and in a spirit God, cannot believe in the miraculous. . . . To say that Christ rose in the body implies that the senses of those people for whom he rose in the body acted irregularly, and contrarily to those relations of the senses which always recur and are accepted by all, and therefore one can only pity the diseased state of these men. But to say that Christ lives spiritually in man, and that we live in others and others in us, is to express the ordinary, unquestionable truth comprehensible to every man who lives in the spirit. That which we have indubitably ascertained concerning the super-sensuous is that, in addition to what we have come to know with our five senses—in addition to having learnt the limits of our being through contact with other beings who surround us—we are inevitably brought to the acknowledgment of the existence of something uncognisable through the senses, but undoubtedly existent. . . . There is, therefore, something besides that which our senses give us, but the existence of which we acknowledge, not because it has been shown to us by any of our senses breaking those laws concerning them which we have deduced and accepted, but on the contrary by our being brought to a recognition of the existence of this by reason; and this recognition not only does not violate the laws of relationship which we have discovered, but, on the contrary, institutes a yet more reasonable connection between these relations.—*Demands of Love and Reason.*

There is one powerful means by which man may more and more clearly know himself and remember who he is. This means is prayer. From the earliest times it has been acknowledged that prayer is necessary to man. For the majority of men prayer was, and still is, an appeal made to a God or Gods, with the object of propitiation—an appeal made under certain circumstances, in certain places, and in special words or acts. The Christian teaching knows nothing of such prayers, but regards prayer as indispensable, not for avoiding material disasters and acquiring material welfare, but for strengthening man in his conflict with sins. . . . Christian prayer is therefore of two kinds: that which elucidates for man his position in the world—occasional prayer; and that which accompanies his every action, bringing it to God's judgment, weighing it—continual prayer.—*The Christian Teaching*.

VI.—THE MEANING OF LIFE

I used to think it impossible to show people their mistake and sin without hurting them. 'Is it possible to pull out a tooth without giving pain? Yes, cocaine and chloroform can allay physical suffering; but there is nothing of the kind for the soul.' Thus I thought, but then immediately said to myself, 'No; there *is* a spiritual chloroform. Here, as in other things, the body has been studied thoroughly, but the soul has not yet been considered. The operation of cutting off a leg or an arm is done with chloroform; whereas the operation of mending a man's soul is done without, and it hurts. That is why it often does not cure, but only causes a worse illness—that of ill-will. And yet there is a spiritual chloroform, and it is well known; it is always love.' And that is not all: it is possible to perform a physical operation satisfactorily without chloroform, but the soul is extremely sensitive, and so every operation performed without the anæsthetic of love must always be disastrous.—*The Root of the Evil.*

It is easy to learn whether there is much iron in the sun, and what other metals there are in the sun and the stars; but it is hard, yes, frightfully hard, to discover that which convicts us of immorality.—*The Kreutzer Sonata.*

Not to see the promised land towards which one has led others, or contributed ever so little to leading others—this is the unchangeable law of true life. The more genuine the work of true life, the more remote are its results; and not only remote but endless are its consequences: therefore we cannot see them. We can foresee more than our generation will witness. A house that is being built we may see, and we may reach the rank of general; but we shall not witness liberation from State slavery, nor even from Land slavery. This is the most evident proof that life consists, not in the realisation of an aim, but in the fulfilment of an embassy.

You will ask: In what does the work accomplished by the life of the universe consist? To this I will answer that we cannot know it all, but can always know when we contribute towards and when we oppose it. Loving relations towards all that lives—first of all, of course, towards men, the nearest of them—the experience of this feeling and of its stimulation in others, is an indication of one's participation in the common work. The experience of the feeling of enmity, hatred, and of its stimulation in others, is an indication of opposition to the common work.

We cannot know God's object, if it were for this reason only—that it is infinite. But we do know, and can always know, whether we are fulfilling His will—that for which we are living, which He desires of us. He holds us, as it were, with reins, and we, like horses, do not know whither we are going, nor wherefore; but we do know, through pain, when we are going whither we ought not; and by a sense of freedom, absence of restraint, when we are going where we should. . . . His will is, in the first place, that we should pay in good works the rent of the life given us. Good works are those which increase love in men. And the work is to augment, cultivate, that talent, our soul, which is also given us. And one cannot do one without the other. One cannot do good works which increase love without augmenting one's talent, one's soul—without increasing love in it; and one cannot augment one's talent, increase love in one's soul, without doing good to men, increasing love in them.

We all think that our duty, our calling, is to fulfil various works: to educate our children, accumulate a fortune, write a book, discover a law of science; but one thing only is necessary—that life should be a complete, good, rational work; a work not in the eyes of men, leaving behind it the memory of a good life, but a work before God: to present to him oneself, one's soul, better than it was, nearer to Him, more submissive to Him, more in conformity. To think thus—above all, to feel thus, is very difficult. One keeps turning off into human glory. But it is possible, and necessary. Help me, God!

Remember that thy life consists only in the fulfilment of the will of God on earth; but to fulfil the will of God is impossible: thou canst only cultivate thy spiritual essence; and cultivate it thou canst only by maintaining purity in thy animal, humility in thy human, and love in thy divine life. For the maintenance of purity, privations are necessary; for humility, bad repute and humiliations; for love, the enmity of men towards thee are necessary. ('And if ye love them that love you, what thanks have ye?') And, therefore, that which thou callest suffering, that which thou complainest of, which troublest thee, which thou regrettest, art afraid of, all this is naught else than either privations and pain; or evil repute, insult, humiliation; or enmity of men towards thee; and the one, the other, and the third are necessary to thee for the maintenance of purity, humility, love; for the cultivation of thy spiritual essence; for the service of the Kingdom of God; for life. And, therefore, I should be not grieved by but glad of privations and humiliations and enmity.

The living man is the one who advances towards that which is illuminated by the lamp moving in front of him and who never reaches the limit of the illuminated space, since it always recedes before him. This is life, and there is no other.

That which we disdain, the immediate realisation in small things of the truth we know, this alone is necessary.

If I were the Tsar's ambassador in Turkey, how I should control myself, watch myself! But being now God's ambassador in the world—I am utterly careless.

And yet a Tsar cannot be aware of all my doings, whereas here it is impossible to conceal anything.

I am still thinking of the evil of choosing an external object for one's life. 'Seek ye first the kingdom of God and his truth, and the rest will be added unto you.' Seaman, be guided by the compass which is on thy ship —by the tiny needle which is a thousand times smaller than the ship—and not by any visible object, not even the stars; all misleads, except that which is in thee!

I threw a chip into a whirlpool, and observed how it spun. A steamer is a similar chip, only a little bigger; the world—a speck; a thousand years—one minute. All is nothing, all that is material is nothing; one thing only is real, unquestionable—the law according to which everything, both small and great, is accomplished—the will of God.

My chief work is not merely to fulfil the five commandments, not merely to denounce property, avoid sin, etc.—all this is not the work, they are only the conditions of the works, complying with which I may be certain that I am realising my calling, they are the forms of my influence on others. My work itself is to live to impart to the world by all the means in my power the element of reason.

That which appears to us as the movement of our personal life is the form our life takes when we place ourselves at an angle with the life of God. But when we place ourselves in the *same* direction, then this life passes through us, we ourselves remaining stationary—

the illusion of personal life disappears and we are conscious that we are, our life is, nothing else than the power of God. . . . But what is this infinite power in its fulness? This is an eternal mystery, and it is not necessary for me to know any more. I know only that in this state death is not fearful. 'Into Thy hands I commend my spirit.' The separateness of my spirit, which was produced by the form through which I was passing, ceases, and I unite with the *all*. I have lately begun to feel this—that when I die I shall not really die, but shall live in all the rest.—*The Meaning of Life.*

In practice the theory or ideal is never perfectly fulfilled; in other words, man never attains perfection, but only approaches towards it. It is impossible to draw a mathematically straight line—all lines are but approximations to the ideal; such incomplete fulfilment of the ideal is the inevitable condition of life, and is not sin—everyone advances towards the ideal according to his powers. But concession, or compromise in theory, is a great sin. If I, knowing that a straight line is a mathematical conception, try to draw one, I shall attain an approximation to a straight line; but if, seeing that it is impossible to draw a perfectly straight line, I decide that I may deviate from the ideal of the straight line, then I stray away, God knows where. It is the same with moral principles.

The question of utility must be altogether set aside by the Christian. No one can decide questions of utility—who will be benefited, and in what way? Utility is beyond our power; but what we should do for the accomplishment of the Father's will—this we know and this we must do. What you say about your activity—about the necessity, or rather advantage of making certain compromises, simply in order that you may be able to continue your activity—does not convince me. The most precious thing you possess, and that you are able to possess, is your soul, your spiritual personality, and this is also the most powerful instrument of your influence over others; therefore, the lowering of your spiritual personality (and every conscious compromise is such a lowering) cannot, for any purpose, be advantageous. I am so alarmed at those customary, pernicious compromises, which deprive life of all its significance, that I challenge this foe everywhere, and attack him, especially when I hear considerations as to the apparent utility we attain.

There is only one way of serving mankind. That is, to become better yourself.—*Letters on the Personal Christian Life.*

VII.—HEREAFTER.

When the divine essence of the soul, which is spiritual, independent of time and space, enclosed in the body in this life—when this divine essence leaves the body, it ceases to be conditioned by time or space, and therefore one cannot say of this essence that it *will be*. It *is*. As Christ said, 'Before Abraham was, I am.' So also with us all. If we are, we always have been, and shall be. We *are*. It is precisely the same with the question: *Where* shall we be? When we say *where*, we speak of a place. But the idea of place is only caused by that condition of separation from all else in which we have been placed. At death this separation will cease, and thus for those still living in this world we shall be everywhere and nowhere. For us locality will not exist.

Therefore no representation of what will be after death gives such an answer as will satisfy a reasonable man. Nor can this be otherwise. The question is wrongly formulated. Humane reason, which can work only in the conditions of time and space, seeks to give an answer concerning that which is outside these conditions. One thing only is known to reason: that the divine essence does exist, that it has been growing while in this world, and that, having attained a certain extent of growth, it has passed out of these conditions.

One thing alone is certain and indubitable, that which Christ said when he was dying, 'Into Thy hands I commend My spirit'; that is to say, at death I return whence I came. And if I believe *that* from which I have emanated to be reason and love (and these two realities I know), then I shall joyously return to Him, knowing that it will be well with me. Not only have I no regret but I rejoice at the thought of the passage which awaits me.—*The Christian Teaching.*

THE END

PRINTED BY
WILLIAM CLOWES AND SONS, LIMITED,
LONDON AND BECCLES.